Words Unbound

Words Unbound

TEACHING DANTE'S INFERNO
IN THE HIGH-SCHOOL CLASSROOM

Milton Burke

THE UNIVERSITY OF ARKANSAS PRESS

FAYETTEVILLE

2017

Text design by Ellen Beeler

⊖ The paper used in this publication meets the minimum requirements of the American National Standard for Permanence of Paper for Printed Library Materials Z39.48-1984.

Library of Congress Control Number: 2017932455

To Mimi

CONTENTS

FOREWORD

In *Words Unbound,* Milton Burke, an experienced high-school teacher of Dante's *Inferno*, offers detailed assistance to those who might wish to teach this text to their students or to those who already teach the text, but might wish some guidance in doing so more effectively. To the best of my knowledge, there is no other book that does this. There are plenty of books on Dante, to be sure, but none specifically written by a high-school teacher for high-school teachers. In fact, the book reads like something of a pedagogical self-help book. The manuscript is divided into sections that track the order of the poem, with a mini-essay in each section offering a brief orientation toward the text and problems a teacher will encounter in it, followed by a series of teaching aids, the kind of material that might appear in a traditional teacher's guide, but in an open-ended and generous-minded spirit. This book doesn't close the text down by presenting answers; it opens it up to exploration and discovery in ways that will inevitably vary from classroom to classroom.

Burke, who has taught *Inferno* for decades, offers straightforward, no-nonsense advice in a voice that is colloquial and occasionally hortatory. He is clearly a master teacher, knowledgeable about his subject matter, but also about what works in the classroom, and by what works, I mean not only what helps students learn Dante, but more importantly what reading Dante can help students learn about themselves and their world. In today's academic environment, what passes for professional development too often involves training in how to administer mandated testing procedures or how to implement the latest legislative initiative or how to accommodate one's syllabus to a prescribed curriculum. This book assumes from the outset that teaching is a noble profession—a vocation—and it summons teachers to be their best selves and to help their students come to understand what their best selves might be. This means that the book has the potential to provide professional development of the most profound type: something that can, for engaged and willing teachers, transform the way they conduct their classes. The focus is on Dante, but the takeaway, the approach, can be applied to the teaching of any subject.

There's no denying that teaching *Inferno* can seem daunting. The text asks a great deal from teacher and student alike. It is intensely, unrelentingly learned, accompanied by footnotes to historical and cultural references that can make it feel alien to any reader, especially a young one. Let me begin, therefore, by reassuring you if you've never taught *Inferno* that, although it's true that the more often you read this work the more you will see in it, it is surprisingly accessible to committed first-time readers, especially if that reading is undertaken in a spirited and supportive learning community. This book is designed to help you reinforce that kind of community. Students recognize this as a "hard" text, but they also recognize it as a culturally and personally important one, and they are flattered their teacher thinks them capable of handling a document of such significance. They are not being patronized, not being condescended to, not being coddled. This text is the real deal, a mature text that deserves its place in our cultural pantheon and it has the power to transform its readers like few others. While I've never taught Dante in high school, I have taught eighteen seminars on Dante for school teachers, and my ongoing interactions with the hundreds of teachers in these programs have provided me an unusual window into what it is like to do so. What these teachers tell me, over and over again, is that teaching Dante is a heady experience, a treat for teacher and student alike, a course that everyone involved anticipates with eagerness and recalls with something akin to reverence.

Before Milton Burke takes you in hand and offers his guidance, I'd like to make a couple of introductory points about *Inferno*, acknowledging as I do so that these are points that he discusses with great subtlety. The first concerns one of the underlying narrative techniques of the entire poem, the differentiation between Dante the pilgrim and Dante the poet, and what this implies about the poem's narrative premise. At its most fundamental level, the *Comedy* traces Dante's physical journey from the dark wood in the first canto of *Inferno* to his direct vision of God in the final canto of *Paradiso*, but saying this raises the question of who this "Dante" is. He is the character who takes the journey, of course, the "pilgrim," but also the voice of the narrator, usually called, by way of contrast, the "poet," who has, in the fiction of the poem, completed the journey and who, therefore, understands its significance in a way that the often-confused pilgrim frequently does not or cannot. This is the basic premise of any first-person conversion narrative: I was not then who I am now, and this is how the change occurred. The result of this narrative posture is that there is frequently an ironic distance between the reactions of the pilgrim, who may not yet be entirely trustworthy in evaluating and responding to the events and characters he encounters, and the poet, who is more likely to reflect the beliefs of the person who actually wrote the *Inferno*. This is a third Dante, but tradition has not conferred a neat and memorable name for him, as with pilgrim and poet. This is Dante the real, flesh-and-blood person who invented both the narrator and the character, as well as the poem's invented environments.

This distinction leads to the unusual narrative premise that I mentioned in the previous paragraph. In the succinct formulation of Charles Singleton, perhaps the most important American Dante scholar of the twentieth century, "the fiction of the *Comedy* is that it is not fiction." The poem asks us to believe that Dante pilgrim really took the journey that Dante poet recounts, and even though we know this is an invention, while we are in the grip of the poem's narrative, it is easy to forget this. And in a sense, this is as it should be. In *The Art of the Novel*, Henry James famously asserts the necessity of granting an artist "his subject, his idea, what the French call his *donnée*," and in Dante's case that means believing (for literary purposes, not as a matter of religious belief) that Dante is negotiating a realm created by God in which the souls of the dead are assigned to specific areas for eternity, with like souls grouped together, based on the values by which they lived. This means that *Inferno* presents a moral geography: where the souls are assigned in Dante's world defines who they are. Several of the souls attempt spirited defenses of their innocence, and Dante pilgrim, who is often presented as a moral work in progress, is sometimes moved to sympathy by their words and fate. We need to recall that within the expressed ground rules of the poem, their location within the afterlife, because it claims to express God's judgment of them, provides a definitive evaluation of their behavior, no matter what they may say to exonerate themselves. The default tone of these self-justifications, in other words, is a species of dramatic irony.

The implied point of saying "the fiction of the poem is that it is not fiction" is to reassert the poem's fictiveness at times when we might be tempted to forget it. In Canto 3, for example, the gate of hell proclaims that justice moved God to exercise his power, wisdom, and love in creating *Inferno*, a region of suffering from which escape is impossible; hence the need to abandon all hope. We all know that no such gate exists except in a fictional world and that this entire fictional world, gate included, is created by Dante, not by God. What the gate proclaims is not a description of anything in the universe, but something essential to Dante's literary enterprise. However, saying that Dante, not God, invented the gate along with the various levels of *Inferno* and the torments described within them doesn't resolve the problem for many readers that the souls we encounter seem to be punished by an unyielding judge, whether that judge be Dante or Dante's God. I'd like to suggest that if this were all that Dante was up to, his poem would scarcely be worth reading except as a historical curiosity. Dorothy Sayers summed the crucial point up nicely in saying that Dante's three volumes present "the drama of the soul's choice." Human freedom is so crucial to Dante and to the God he presents that people are left radically free to make any moral choice they wish in their lives. Those who choose to pursue self-destructive or antisocial or duplicitous behavior, are free to do so, but then they go on doing so in *Inferno*, where any self-deception they may have practiced in explaining away their behavior is stripped bare so that they—and we as readers—confront, in a series of metaphorically appropriate environments, the reality of their earthly behavior.

The term used to describe this situation is *contrapasso*, a term used by Dante himself as the final word of Canto 28 of *Inferno*. Literally, it means countersuffering, and because no analogous word exists in English, Dante scholars traditionally have simply adopted Dante's own term. The underlying notion can be traced back to the early days of Christianity, namely that sin so distorts the reality of who we are as human beings that the real punishment for sin is sin itself. God doesn't put these souls in hell; they put themselves in hell by their behavior and they had already done so while they were still alive, even though this may be difficult for the casual observer to recognize. Their circumstance after death is merely an extension of this status, a confirmation in the afterlife externalizing and objectifying the way they were already living. In *Inferno*, that is, their earthly behavior is not so much punished as revealed. The function of the punishment, as Dante Pilgrim will learn in the central canto of *Paradiso*, is pedagogical. If you want an analogy that's close to home, it's like saying you don't give your students grades; you simply record the grades they've given themselves. (You might be advised, however, not to try this notion out on your students.) As you encounter the various groups in *Inferno*, you will want to tease out the implications of the contrapasso for each, and this book does an excellent job of helping you do so.

The final point I'd like to make takes us back to the inscription over the gate of hell. In *Paradiso*, Dante makes clear that he understands that God is beyond human categories and anything we say about him inevitably needs to resort to figurative language to reduce his radical otherness to terms humans can comprehend. One example can be found in the previous sentence where I used male pronouns to refer to God (a practice I'll continue, if only for the sake of convenience). In *Paradiso* 4, we're told that the Bible speaks of God's hands and feet as a way of "condescending" to human understanding. To say, as the gospels do, that Christ sits at the right hand of God or to say, as Isaiah does, that heaven is God's throne and earth is his footstool does not mean anyone believes God has hands and feet, any more than God has gender. Dante understands we project human characteristics onto God by analogy, to make the discussion of God possible, however imperfectly. The anthropomorphizing on Dante's hell gate projects onto God the human ideals of justice, power, wisdom, and love. We project onto God as divine attributes that we most admire in ourselves. These qualities are fundamental to all people, but perhaps especially so to teenagers, who are in the process of defining and refining the core of their moral selves.

To expand upon this, I'd make the point, again drawing upon what teachers have told me, that students find *Inferno* "relevant," and, I would add, with good cause. It's not a given that this should be so, since the plot involves characters Dante meets in thirteenth-century Italy and the text is suffused with allusions to a wide range of classical and medieval literary and historical sources. But it doesn't take students long to realize that the issues Dante addresses engage many of their own passions and concerns, starting with the poem's first lines: in the middle of the journey of his life, Dante finds he has lost his way and is in a metaphorical dark wood. It's the rare teenager who can't empathize with the pilgrim's sense of dread and alienation, while the poem's ongoing and continuous engagement of the theme of conversion provides a lifeline of hope to those who wonder if their spiritual, moral, and emotional lives can, in fact, be transformed. In our culture, we're likely to think of conversion as switching from one religion to another, but in Dante's world conversion retains its etymological force (turning with) and involves turning away from the anxiety and guilt we feel when we know we've strayed from our moral center and toward a reintegration with the path in life that we know to be its true trajectory. It's not an easy spiritual or moral movement for Dante to undertake. It requires guidance, in *Inferno* primarily from Virgil, and is subject to frequent errors of judgment by Dante pilgrim as he encounters the souls he meets on his journey. But we know from the poem's title that we're dealing with a comedy, and we know the last volume will take us to paradise, so whatever backsliding Dante may suffer, we can be confident we're tracking a story of moral growth. And if you can tolerate a spoiler, what Dante learns in *Paradiso* is that he is called upon to be a prophet, not in the sense of one who predicts the future, but as someone called upon to speak truth to power, to call upon his readers to engage in personal reform, and upon society to reshape itself in accordance with the stated ideals from which it too often strays. As such, Dante is embracing a fundamentally heroic attitude, one that students will recognize as a summons to moral courage.

Part of what Dante is learning in *Inferno* are the various insidious ways in which personal and social evil can manifest themselves and the ways in which they destroy personal happiness and communal justice. The sinners Dante encounters during his journey force readers to consider the nature of a wide range of concerns that are no less urgent today than they were seven centuries ago. Love and sex, political corruption and bribery, the violation of public service, greed, partisan hostility, cynicism, white-collar crime—all of these may be inflected differently in Dante's world, but their persistence in ours will be immediately recognizable to your students. Young people often share these concerns in a particularly intense way and teachers may feel that it's important for them to reinforce their concerns for the good of our students and our country.

It's hard to do so, however, without becoming preachy, and this brings me to what I consider to be one of the strongest aspects of *Words Unbound*: how to engage student discussion of the controversial issues that have so divided our nation. In the early pages of the book, Burke discusses the importance of straddling the barriers that divide our students and working to break them down. The deep divisions in our country, highlighted by the culture wars, can be traced back for decades, but that split is highlighted increasingly by the prevalence of social media and the algorithms that funnel material to us in an ideological monotone. After the 1972 election, Pauline Kael, the *New Yorker* film critic, famously said that she knew only one person who had voted for Richard Nixon. That kind of cultural isolation has grown in intensity as apps like Facebook track the sites we click on and send increasingly focused links to our inboxes and news feeds. The more we click, the more revenues the app receives, and so the app increases the flow of "news" that reinforces our presuppositions and vilifies those of "outsiders." Such a cultural environment undermines introspection and thoughtful reflection about one's own values, while trivializing and vilifying those of one's "opponents." Those quotation marks in the last two sentences are there because clearly this should not be the way we think about issues, about the sources of our information on political and cultural affairs, or about our neighbors, but there is precious little in our culture to counter this seemingly ever-present barrage of "information." One of the most important aspects of *Words Unbound* is Burke's passionate appeal that the place to engage in such discussion can be the classroom—and the Dante classroom in particular. The teaching profession is more central to our communal health than ever. We all know this, and this book provides practical suggestions for taking part in that process.

One last point. Whether you're considering offering a Dante course for the first time or have already done so, you'll be interested to know that The Dante Society of America, the country's most prestigious scholarly organization dedicated to the life and works of the poet, has added to its support of traditional scholarship on Dante a new commitment to education and outreach through its website: https://www.dantesociety.org/education-and-outreach. Among the links on that site, you will find information on the Durling Prize, awarded annually to a teacher of Dante, and "Student Encounters," an online anthology of high-school student writings on Dante. These are exciting times for the teaching of Dante, and this book provides a wealth of guidance for those who wish to join in the fun.

William A. Stephany
University of Vermont

ACKNOWLEDGMENTS

Thanks to the NEH for a grant years ago that gave me the chance to study the *Divine Comedy* full time for a year. I also want to thank those who read all or part of my manuscript and offered helpful suggestions toward improving it: Mimi Burke, Massey Burke, Tom Cochran, and especially Bob Cochran and Bill Stephany.

INTRODUCTION

I'm writing this book to help remedy a deficiency: the relative absence of Dante in the syllabi of high-school literature classes. Few writers of his stature appear there less than he. This situation is lamentable because Dante's *Commedia* has so much to offer high school students, particularly in this age. I want to do what I can to rectify this situation. Though I can't help referring to the *Commedia* as a whole at times, this book concerns the teaching of *Inferno*, the first of the three major divisions of the poem and certainly the one most accessible to high-school students.

Two primary assumptions underlie this study: that what you teach is as important as how you teach, and that the quality of your teaching of a given work is contingent upon how much you know about it. In general, the more you have studied and reflected on a work, the better you will teach it. Neither premise is pedagogically fashionable these days, but I could cite experience, history, and good sense to defend both.

I'm writing mainly for teachers entrenched in the pitched battle for the minds of modern students, that is, to all high-school literature teachers. This book is then a pragmatist's offer to his classroom kin. It is the effect of thirty years of experience teaching Dante's *Inferno* to public high-school students in Arkansas. Readers seeking a scholarly approach to Dante's work will be disappointed. (This is not at all to deny the value of *Commedia* scholarship. My own study of the poem has been greatly enriched by some of that work. My favorite edition of *Inferno* is Robert and Jean Hollanders' [2008], arguably the most scholarly single volume one available.) I am at best an experienced Dante amateur, limited in expertise but in love with the game. Armed with a little Latin, I can stumble through Dante's tercets in Italian, given enough time and an Italian-English dictionary at my elbow. Though often rewarding, such laborious plodding is hardly the mark of a Dante scholar. But I assume that high-school teachers are not looking primarily for help from academic specialists, though at many points that might be beneficial. You want guidance from someone more like you, perhaps more knowledgeable than you are in this literary area, but familiar from long experience with your situation and the pressures you face. You'll want to hear in mine a colleague's voice.

Any good edition of *Inferno* will provide a wealth of introductory information, filling in some of the poem's historical and biographical background. For a literary world as exotic as Dante's is likely to seem to your students, that's crucial. They will need some orientation. *Inferno* introductions cover the spectrum from purely informational to primarily interpretive. The one to John Ciardi's (2001) edition, for example, leans toward the former, the one by the Hollanders toward the latter. Teaching *Inferno* well probably hinges on the close reading of some such authoritative body of introductory material. But since so much of what I say below depends on some prior knowledge about poet and poem, I should sketch in a few essentials here.

The *Commedia* was written by Dante Alighieri, a Florentine poet and political figure who lived from 1265 to 1321. This was a time of protracted and intense civil strife in his region of Italy, and in Florence particularly. Because of a political power shift in Florence in 1302, Dante was exiled, never to return. He spent the last two decades of his life finding out "how salt is the taste of another man's bread, how hard is the way up and down another man's stairs" (*Paradiso* 17:58–60). Writing from a patron's home, he began the *Commedia* in about 1305, finishing it only shortly before his death. Like several of the world's greatest pieces of literature, then, his poem was conditioned by the experience of exile. The implications of that are worth pondering.

Readers who expect a purely religious poem might be surprised at the encyclopedic political, scientific, historical, geographical, and cultural commentary it contains. Still, no story could be more fundamentally Christian in its ultimate concern. It follows the journey of a spiritually struggling protagonist, Dante himself in the year 1300 at age thirty-five, in the middle of his life's journey. In the course of the poem's one hundred cantos, the protagonist makes his way as a living being through the three lands of the dead: inferno, purgatory and paradise. These also constitute the three main divisions, or canticles, of the *Commedia*. By the end of the *Commedia*, the protagonist, pathetically abject when the poem begins, has ascended from the depths of hell up the mountain of purgatory through the upper reaches of paradise, finally to look upon the pinpoint of light that is what human beings can perceive of God. At this point, we infer, the poor pilgrim has matured enough to go back to the world and write the great poem.

Hence Dante's original title: the *Commedia* (*Divina* was added to the title by later editors). Though Dante occasionally does express his sense of humor in the poem, it is a comedy primarily in its traditional literary sense: a narrative that ends happily. That definition fits the *Commedia,* but in an almost laughably understated way. Happiness hardly seems adequate to the direct experience of God's paradisal light. According to Northrop Frye's (2000) *Anatomy of Criticism*, comedy should be seen as a socially integrative literary form, with the hero ultimately being incorporated, often reincorporated, into the larger social order. Substitute cosmic for social and you approach the vision accorded the pilgrim in the poem's last few lines:

> But now my will and my desire, like wheels revolving
> With an even motion, were turning with
> The Love that moves the sun and all the other stars. (*Paradiso* 33:143–45)

You can't be integrated more grandly than that.

Did the historical Dante actually experience something like the events recorded in the *Commedia*? It is safe to say critical opinion is divided on this question. One's answer probably depends on how he understands "something like." I find it hard to take Dante's hundred-canto journey literally to any degree at all because the terrain he covers is just too neatly arranged. You won't read long before discovering how much order governs God's constructions in the poem. This is reflected in Dante's obvious partiality to numerical symbolism. The *Commedia* comprises three canticles composed of thirty-three cantos each, which, together with *Inferno*'s initial introductory canto, total an even one hundred. Each canticle is graded into major subdivisions—circles, terraces, spheres—which are then, especially in *Inferno*, further subdivided. Symmetries abound both within and between canticles. The nine sinful circles of hell, for example, parallel neatly the nine blessed spheres of heaven. Dante thus presses the idea of divine order about as far as a piece of literature can without seeming mechanical. In the fourteenth century, he must have found a lot of theological backing for his poem's numerological patterns, with the number three predominating. But you don't have to buy number mysticism to credit Dante's larger point: God creates orderly structures because structure conveys intelligibility. It is order that human beings can understand, historically, scientifically and, particularly in *Inferno*, morally. You should read Dante's journey through *Inferno*, at least primarily, as an education in the logic of moral choices and their consequences. I'm guessing that at some critical midlife point the historical Dante really did undergo something like this education.

Dante the poet chooses Virgil, the great Roman poet, as his pilgrim's guide through *Inferno*. This choice was the first thing that got a secularist like me interested in the poem, and it epitomizes the quality that continues to intrigue me most. All the circles and levels that catch human souls after death could come to seem static, mechanical, and confining, were it not for something in Dante's view of things that strains against his own intricately drawn boundaries. What's a Roman poet doing as the guide through the afterlife in a Christian epic? Why is a Roman pagan suicide stationed at the base of the Mount of Purgatory, from which position, we assume, he will eventually ascend to paradise? Why are Muslim philosophers in Limbo while the founder of their religion suffers among the schismatics deep in hell? A careful reading of the poem is bound to generate many such questions. Provocative exceptions to Dante's categorizations abound. However strongly codified God's forms of order in the *Commedia* seem, Dante's God is no legalist. That, to me, can make this poem accessible to all your students, not just intellectually but in matters of the heart. Dante's embrace turns out to be much wider than you might think.

This suggests my main reason, among many, for urging you to include *Inferno* in your courses. Managing discussion in a high-school literature class puts you in the (ultimately) enviable position of straddling the barriers that divide your students. This work can break down those barriers. Christian/secularist, conservative/liberal, iconoclast/traditionalist, and, if you will allow it, student/teacher: all such simplistic oppositions can wither in the heat of good *Inferno* discussion. By the early 1980s, I could see that the culture wars were having no trouble finding their way into my classroom. In emulation of their elders perhaps, my students were taking increasing pleasure in sharpening their differences with those around them. Building high the barricades of separation was, in its usual defensive, unhealthy way, satisfying a need, maybe *the* need, what Tobias Wolff (1995) calls "the sensation of occupying a safe place in a coherent scheme" (5). I came to see the dismantling of such walls as one of the greatest benefits of reading and discussing serious literature and as the high-school literature teacher's weightiest task. I found myself constructing my syllabus around that primary concern. Paradoxically, given that it is so full of boundaries, Dante's poem became one of my most effective tools in the struggle to accomplish that aim. How that could be this book hopes to show.

You'll make headway in this rewarding direction to the degree that you can convince your students to read with as much objectivity and charity as they can muster. Without these two pillars of support, any serious high-school literature project will totter. Your students' first concern should be to construe as sympathetically as the language will allow what a writer thinks and how he came to think that way. Short of that, they haven't really been, as we literature teachers like to say, exposed to a writer. In sustaining these reading virtues, they will need your frequent encouragement. Urge them to bracket their own assumptions while they are trying to understand Dante's mind. After they have thoroughly chewed on Dante's thinking as reflected in *Inferno*, there will be plenty of time to digest him in their own juices. And, one hopes, vice-versa.

To avoid endless tedious qualifications, I will express many claims in this book more unreservedly than they warrant. Even a cursory look at some *Commedia* commentary will show how broad a spectrum of interpretation this poem can spawn. Up front then, please allow me one comprehensive "I think" to cover all my interpretive and experiential pronouncements in this book, and all my imperatives. I hope you don't see this as a weakness. The willingness to qualify my judgments about a text served me well in the high-school classroom. It was part of a two-pronged approach. For any work I taught, I would work hard to come up with as coherent and comprehensive an interpretation as possible and to defend it in class discussion as we went. I think that was effective because it gave my students a perspective against which to react. And react they certainly would. Then I would have to be ready to modify my positions under whatever criticisms, refutations, and proposed revisions they came up with, as long as they were consistent with the text. Dealing with the demands this strategy makes on the teacher as authority figure was definitely a struggle for me, but I learned a lot by not shrinking from that. I wouldn't now think of teaching literature in any other way.

Call this the provisional approach to the teaching of literature. You'll notice that I try to use it in this book as well. Whatever the merits of the interpretive positions I take here, I'll be happier if they help prompt you to frame your own approach to teaching *Inferno* than if you unblinkingly treat them as truth.

The "Exercises" sections at the end of each chapter highlight some topics from the selected cantos that I have found productive of meaningful discussion and research. I realize that your schedules may not leave you time to entertain in class more than a fraction of them, but better too many possibilities than too few. You'll notice that I often fill much space in framing my questions. That's because experience tells me it can take a lot of work to set up a good question for your students. But I'm more intent here on sketching in areas worth exploring than laying out fully developed lessons or activities. You'll have to decide whether and how to apply these exercises in your classroom. I ultimately hope they will fertilize the growth of your own good questions and other inventive ways to engage students in the text. In this poem maybe more than any other, it would be hard to exhaust the possible lines of fruitful inquiry. (For some helpful examples of creative activities, see the first three websites listed in appendix 2.)

All quotations are from the Hollanders' *Inferno*. In the appendix, I discuss briefly some other editions of *Inferno* that might be suitable for classroom use.

Words Unbound

1

Two Dantes

CANTO 1

Dante is one of the greatest of literary architects, and the *Commedia* is his masterpiece. If a good book is one that begs to be read again, then Dante's poem may stand supreme. It can sustain any number of rereadings, each one enriching your understanding of what literary structure at its most intricate can convey. Each time through, you find yourself discovering new rooms, new passageways from room to room and wing to wing, more complex design motifs of image, metaphor, language, and sound. Like an architect of the organic school, Dante built the *Commedia* out of local material, the vernacular Italian, shaped to a structure well-suited to the medieval Catholic landscape in which it was set. His building stones consisted primarily of a variety of parallels and contrasts. When you think about it, this could hardly be otherwise. A writer like Dante can only *rely* on meanings generated by relationships internal to his work. He builds these up inside a given work in meaningful patterns of similarity and difference. These two supports bear a great deal of intellectual and emotional weight in this poem. A wealth of beneficial struggle lies in store for your students as they try to grasp how, out of such fundamental materials, Dante constructs *Inferno*, the first section of the surpassingly elegant cathedral that is the *Commedia*.

The basic design of the poem seems very simple. The entire poem evolves out of the relationship between two versions of Dante Alighieri as that develops fictionally over a week at Eastertime in 1300. I'll follow established practice in designating them Dante the pilgrim and Dante the poet. Through much of the *Inferno*, they contrast strongly. The poem depicts Dante the pilgrim, the protagonist of the poem, as a historical figure, thirty-five years of age, living in the year 1300 in Florence, Italy. As a prominent poet and political figure in Florence at the time, he must have seemed to be at the top of his game. But this Dante is paradoxically characterized early in the poem as so diseased in spirit as to be almost beyond help. Dante the poet, on the other hand, has made the journey through hell, purgatory, and paradise, received an education along the way from three exemplary guides, seen a bit of the divine light, and come back to the world ready to give poetic shape to his experiences. The resulting one hundred cantos of the poem gauge the diminishing distance between the two Dantes as the pilgrim gradually develops into the poet. Dissociation gradually moves toward identity. It is important to point out that both of these Dantes are literary creations. How closely either corresponds to the actual Dante, whatever that means, would be hard to determine.

With this essential distinction in mind, have your students begin with a close look at the poem's first few lines. Greek and Roman epic poets typically used these lines to lay a foundation in tone, situation, character, and theme. Dante's first twelve lines in canto 1 continue this tradition. Ask your students to look for anything that might be thematic, but especially for moves that begin to characterize the contrast between the two Dantes. Some significant features they might notice there:

1. Two different verb tenses, the past for the poet's recounting of the
   pilgrim's actions in 1300; the present for the poet's more experienced
   comments on the action in his own voice some time later as he composes the poem. Your students who know a little Spanish or Latin
   might notice how Dante convolutes his word order in the second
   tercet, possibly to highlight the distinction between two times, by
   juxtaposing past and present tense forms of the verb "to be" (era e`).
2. The differing levels of experience between the poet-narrator and
   the pilgrim. From his vantage point in the future, the poet has a
   reflective handle on how things stand for the pilgrim in 1300, how
   the journey will go, and what its significance is. Having barely
   awakened from a deadly sleep, the pilgrim doesn't know much
   about the terrain in which he finds himself. He needs an education.
3. The strong contrast in how the poem evaluates the respective positions of the two Dantes (fearfully lost in a dark, savage place versus
   speaking from a position where things have "come to good").
4. The reflexive verb in the second line (mi ritrovai, which the
   Hollanders translate "I came to myself," maybe more literally "I
   found myself again"). Thus the poem immediately places the same
   person as both subject and object of a verb. The implication is of a
   self, or soul, that is divisible into conceptually discrete parts. This
   idea echoes a long tradition in the West, going back literarily at
   least to Plato's three-part soul in the Republic. You will see that the

structure of hell reflects Dante's own version of the tripartite soul concept.

Critical to Dante's understanding of the path to God is the idea that all humans have better and worse angels of their natures. Pilgrimages like this one are for learning to think and act according to the better ones. The pilgrim can do that in part by facing up to the others, as if they were separable parts of himself, at least potentially. The pilgrim's tour of hell will have to demonstrate how this works. So the first verb in the poem prefigures a critical feature of Dantean psychology: the multipartite self.

5. Language that complicates a little the relation between the two Dantes. No simplistic before-and-after picture can square with the poem's first few lines. The poet still experiences in full force the fear the pilgrim felt. This renders precarious any distance the poet has achieved from his benighted younger self. The poet's memories can still be affected by prior emotional conditioning, so he does not always succeed in maintaining his elevated stance of knowing detachment from the action. It is important to remember that the poet is also given a literary characterization.

Once you start engaging the actual language of the poem, you will see right away that no such list as the above can be exhaustive. You and your students will certainly find more to say about the opening lines. This poem everywhere rewards good close reading. For a literature teacher, that's one of its beauties.

I have intentionally refrained from mentioning until now the poem's famous first line. *Nostra vita. Our* journey. In what sense "our"? How can the poet claim universality for a pilgrim's experiences, which are highly individualized in place, time, character, and situation? Attempting to answer that question can deliver you pretty quickly into the mire of allegorical interpretations of the poem. For those unfamiliar with the form, allegory entails two or more parallel planes of narrative: a literal level and one or more symbolic ones linked to the literal in one-to-one correspondence, more or less. To read the critics on allegory in this poem was for me a process of deepening bewilderment, so complex were the issues and varied the interpretations. Dante can be held somewhat responsible for any such confusion. A still extant letter to his patron Can Grande (Toynbee 1920) outlines four levels at which his poem can be read, one literal and three allegorical. I have yet to find a commentary dealing with more than a detail or two in the poem at all four levels. You would save yourself and your students a lot of trouble by simply skirting this morass, but that would be beating a coward's retreat. Besides, Dante's first line seems designed to close off that avenue of escape. Implicit in that "our" is Dante's insistence from the start that allegorical thinking is critical to understanding the poem. The *Inferno* will certainly reward your students' thoughtful effort expended on this problem.

The entire first canto seems designed to reinforce this point. Throughout most of *Inferno*, the poet foregrounds the historically anchored story of a certain Florentine pilgrim's progress. The pilgrim continually encounters Italians who know him personally or who have played some significant part in cultural or political events in contemporary Italy. You are so frequently sent running to the footnote page for information on thirteenth-century Italian figures and events that you initially have to read literally to read at all. This is as it should be. What distinguishes Dante's poem structurally from other narrative poetry of his day is not allegory itself. Medieval literature bristled with that. But Dante refuses to demote the literal story in favor of allegorical abstractions. How does a poet tell a story full of richly individualized characters and images while at the same time giving those details representational force? Dante's *Commedia* surely constitutes one of literature's most perfectly realized solutions to this perennial artistic problem. This poem distinguishes itself in the way that literal and allegorical work together in it. Among other things, this suggests that to do justice to the *Inferno*, you first have to read it literally.

But that will prove harder with the first canto than the others. Echoing that "our," the poem's first images and beings push you forcefully beyond the letter. A dark wood so bitter that death isn't more so? A timely little hill waiting with upper slopes bathed in light from a source "that leads men straight, no matter what their course"? Progress arrested by three beasts, the last of which is explicitly associated with appetites that cause widespread human malaise? Just the right guide appearing from nowhere at a critical moment? Your students will have a hard time staying literal about such images. They seem designed to establish from the start an allegorical dimension to the poem.

But what dimension? Though I can't claim to understand much of the critical conversation about allegory in the poem, I can propose a way of dealing with the problem that has made the poem more accessible to me personally and has worked well with my students over the years. Let Dante the pilgrim be himself in historical time and simultaneously any soul in any age. That is, first think of the pilgrim's journey as that of a thirteenth-century Florentine poet and political figure through the lands of the dead and then as a representation of any soul's inward movement toward the light. Literally, then, hell, purgatory, and paradise categorize destinations of human souls after death; allegorically they represent territories in the timeless landscape of every human soul.

Working out some method of dealing with allegory in the poem is part of the larger struggle to understand the poem's architecture. To Dante, the keynote to God's creation is structure: no attentive reader will get far in *Inferno* before noticing how ordered the place is. God has structured both our inner and outer worlds to give meaning to human experience and especially to human choice-making. If no structure, Dante in effect maintains, then no meaning. So Dante uses allegory to establish a structural connection between the soul and God's cosmos writ large. He makes it a principal means of revealing the meaningfulness that suffuses divine creation.

Like the pilgrim, your students will have to work hard to understand in detail how God's structure functions in *Inferno* and why he has it this way. They'll get their education in this as the pilgrim gets his. But a few general points should be made at the outset. In Dante's Christian schema, God grants humans limited freedom. They are free to choose but bound to experience the moral consequences of their choices. Unrepented bad choices will lead to malaise, and perhaps not just in the next life. Better choices, or genuine repentance for bad ones, can lead to a better situation. Hell, purgatory, and paradise give spatial and visual expression to this causality, literally as actual places, allegorically as a spectrum of states of inner being from damnable to blessed.

In *Inferno*, the pilgrim gets a very vivid and detailed education in how divine cause and effect works. Dante's hell catalogs in graded detail the negative possibilities open to the kind of choice-making creatures God has shaped us to be. In addition to their literal historicity, the human characters Dante meets in the poem represent specific faculties or kinds of moral/spiritual choosing that are available to all humans by virtue of what a human being is. Inherent in any of us is the possibility, with considerable biological force behind it, of choosing to lead a lust-driven life like Francesca in canto 5, or to adopt a materialist perspective like Farinata (*Inferno* 10), or like Ulysses (*Inferno* 26) to misuse our gifts in serving our own needs to the detriment of others, or to cannibalize the lives around us like Ugolino (*Inferno 33*). All these characters are at once depictions of actual historical or literary figures and allegorical representations of features, dimensions, and tendencies in every soul, the pilgrim and your students not excluded. Tell your students Francesca lives in them — "Close, close, close!" as Simon learns from the beast in *Lord of the Flies* (Golding 1954, 142). That might take their minds off their cell phones a little.

But they also contain something of the pilgrim. In addition to his historical self, Dante the pilgrim represents the soul as still capable of modification. This distinguishes him from the shades he meets in hell, all of whom have lost the power to change their shape morally and must therefore languish in specific forms of eternal torment. The pilgrim still maintains (but just barely, as canto 2 makes clear) the ability to change. He is the educable self, that power in anyone to wake up, step back reflectively to take an honest look at himself, accept guidance, and make new choices that are not simply expressions of old patterns. At his best he is the self you want your students to bring to class every day. But the poet doesn't romanticize this faculty. The pilgrim can't always view things from a comfortable distance. His reflection is subject to obstruction by emotional patterns—habits, fears, compulsions, aversions, scores to settle, and so on. It would be hard to maintain that some such set of conditioned reactions is not eventually etched into every human soul. Even today in class, a few of your students were thumbing those cell phones under their desks.

I think something like this approach can be maintained throughout the *Inferno*, thus satisfying the definition of allegory. Reading this way has many potential benefits. Most importantly, it can make the poem not just accessible but sharply pertinent to a lot more of your students than just the formally Christian ones. Even your most devout secularists might find themselves pulled in by a poem read simultaneously at both these levels. I was.

In a poem that can overwhelm you with complexity of design, the pilgrim/poet contrast and the literal/allegorical parallel are architecturally fundamental. On their foundation, robust class discussion may easily rise. Operate on the premise that your students already have plenty of experience by which to unpack the images in the first canto, all of which represent in spatial form conditions or dimensions of a human soul. Your students can (and will aloud in class, I'm betting) give personal shape to the idea of being in a "dark wood." They have some vision of where they should be as persons, up there on a lighted height. They know that little hill. Given some time to reflect, they will be able to identify those beasts that block their progress toward the light. They will be able to frame a personal response to Virgil's (taunting?) question to the pilgrim in the story: "Why do you not climb the peak that gives delight, origin and cause of every joy?" (1:77–78). They might even be able to distinguish among their own inner voices the measured cadences of a reliable guide.

Which is not to imply that Dante doesn't endorse specific referents for these images. The dark wood springs from Christian ideas about sin and consequent separation from God (whom Dante associates with light throughout the poem). The little lighted hill suggests the Mount of Purgatory, the medieval Catholic pathway to heaven. The beasts reflect the tripartite division of the soul originating in classical antiquity. Understanding Dante's Virgil would require some grounding in classical thought and art, with particular knowledge of Virgil's *Aeneid*, which Dante knew well and to which he often alludes in the *Commedia*. None of this specified content should be neglected. My claim is that it is not intended to be exhaustive. Beyond these specifics, the poem can take on a life with your students that encourages them to shape Dante's journey to their own experience. A kid doesn't have to be a Christian to be interested in doing that.

So your job, if you accept my suggestion, is to help your students form a coherent picture comprising all the elements in canto 1 as a story about a famous Florentine poet and at the same time as features, potentials, or tendencies in every human soul. (Dante's God puts a lot of emphasis on coherence.) Attention to architecturally prominent parallels and contrasts will help you do this. I think your students will find what they should expect from a great writer—a picture of what a human being is that sets them to thinking in ways they haven't before. They are not likely to encounter anywhere a more intricate specimen of literary construction.

Exercises

CLOSE READING

1. How do the first twelve lines of canto 1 prepare the reader for what is to come in the poem? More specifically, how do those lines set up the fundamental contrast between the two Dantes? What lines or images in the rest of the canto start to develop that contrast?

2. The most frequently recurring word in canto 1 is *paura*, fear, which appears five times. Apparently to Dante, fear constitutes a primary obstacle to movement toward the light. This must have applied to Dante personally, and it no doubt threatens to impede spiritual progress for any human soul in some fashion. So why all the emphasis on fear? What is the relation in the canto between fear and the dark wood? Judging by the word's specific uses in the text, what particular kinds of fear is Dante emphasizing? It would be hard to find a theme with more staying power than this one. As someone who has probably accumulated a lot more emotional data than your students, you are in a better position than they to appreciate the truth of this. But events in a terror-stricken world like ours should have seeded even youthful minds with awareness of the subterranean power of undigested fears. They can strike deep roots.

3. Even in canto 1, arguably the most insistently allegorical canto in *Inferno*, Dante's interest in vivid, specific details should be apparent. Ask your students to find examples of details in this canto that seem to carry little or no weight in developing the themes of Dante's particular or the soul's universal journey. They should try to draw conclusions, provisionally since they have just started the poem, about what other interests might govern Dante's artistic choices.

4. One figure of speech that Dante exploits throughout the poem is the epic simile. This is another device that asks your students to think

comparatively. Like other similes, epic ones are comparisons between two things, sometimes termed the vehicle and the tenor. The vehicle is the image the poet introduces into the poem as a comparison to the tenor, the element of the poem to be illuminated. What distinguishes this kind of simile in *Inferno* is its length and regularity of form (vehicle and tenor often running to several lines each, counterbalanced in length and structure; vehicle preceding tenor; formalized comparison-signaling conjunctions often beginning each part, traditionally translated *as* and *so* respectively). Reflecting classical sources, especially Virgil's *Aeneid*, Dante fills his *Commedia* with similes of this kind. Have your students look closely at the poem's initial instance of this device, the shipwreck simile at *Inferno* 1:22–27. Here's the Hollanders' translation of it:

> As one who, with laboring breath,
> has escaped from the deep to the shore
> turns and looks back at the perilous waters,
>
> so my mind, still in flight,
> turned back to look once more upon the pass
> no mortal being ever left alive.

The interpretive question of course entails comparison: how do parallels between vehicle and tenor serve to enrich your understanding of the tenor? In this case, the vehicle characterizes a shipwreck survivor who has just escaped from drowning. At what points does that description parallel the tenor: the pilgrim's situation, having barely managed to wake up to and escape from his life's gathering darkness? Like everything else in the *Commedia*, this device is used with great precision and intricacy. Seemingly trivial details in the vehicle might swell to significance under your students' reflective gaze. I think it is critical to dwell at least occasionally on devices like this to give students a chance to steep themselves in a great writer's artistry. I'm betting they don't get much time to do that in these accountable days.

Possible areas of implication in this simile: something about the gravity of Dante's situation and the narrowness of his escape, about the importance of turning back to face the danger rather than submitting to the impulse to flee, or about the effort required to escape from problems of the dark wood's magnitude. Your students will come up with more to say. That's the on-the-ground beauty of this poem: its implications are so often hard to exhaust. As with any work, your challenge is to help your students shape their immediate responses to the text into a coherent reading of the poem as a whole. Intricate as this poem is, that will constitute no small accomplishment.

5. Dante's other major literary device, also based on parallel thinking, is the allusion. The *Commedia* burgeons with allusions reflecting the poet's knowledge of both Christian and classical sources. His two primary sources would have to be the Bible and Virgil's *Aeneid*. Dante's frequent use of this device can enliven the study of his text almost endlessly for anyone who wants to look up his references and reflect on them. Most English editions of the poem will help you to spot some of Dante's allusions, but by far the best source for hunting them down is Charles Singleton's (1990) line-by-line commentary on the poem.

    Structurally, allusions are like similes. To unpack any allusion, your students must consider how knowledge of the material referred to, usually from another piece of literature, deepens their understanding of the *Inferno* passage where the allusion occurs. You might have your students consider those that occur just in the poem's first tercet. Singleton cites biblical sources for equating a position midway in life's journey with Dante's age of thirty-five in 1300 and for the image of the straight way. For the dark wood, he cites two sources in Virgil's *Aeneid*. For now, you might just ask your students about the significance of summoning these two sources of background material in the first of hundreds of allusions. Whatever else this question might accomplish, it makes a nice transition into a consideration of Dante's take on Virgil and the other great pagan poets and philosophers.

THEMES AND ISSUES

1. How does the poem's basic allegory work if you assume the places and details of the poem correspond to faculties, potentials, or dimensions in every human soul? To read the *Inferno* intelligently, your students really need a clear exposition in their mental notebook of the basic allegorical correspondences in the poem. That makes parallelism fundamental.

2. Why did Dante choose to write his greatest work in the humble Italian vernacular? In his day Latin was, of course, the language of scholarship, and Dante's artistic and philosophical mastery of that language was well established by the time he began his *Commedia*. Because long narrative poems on lofty topics were typically composed in elevated language, level of style conventions would also seem to dictate Latin for this poem. So you might ask your students to speculate on the reasons behind Dante's surprising choice. (Maybe it has the same source as his refusal to subordinate

individual humans to allegorical abstractions: his desire to flesh out this work.)

3.   There is a great historical irony in the pilgrim's situation. In worldly terms, Dante Alighieri stood at the top of Fortune's wheel in 1300. He was already a renowned poet and had been chosen one of the seven priors of Florence. Yet this is the year to which the dismal imagery of the first canto applies. A more obvious setting for the dark wood would have been a couple of years later, when political conflict in Florence had forced Dante into an exile from which he would never return. Your students might discuss the implications of Dante's choice to set the poem when he does.

2

Pagans

CANTOS 1 AND 2

Consider how your genetic makeup affects who you are and how you behave. How much do you really know about that? If you are like me, you have very little immediate awareness of how genes condition your day-to-day experience. Isn't there an analogy here with the influence of classical civilization on Western ways of life? Westerners are taught that we owe a lot of who we are, individually and collectively, to Greek and Roman antiquity. But I doubt that many of us have any clear understanding of the nature of that debt. We don't notice such conditioning because it is part of the faculty by which we notice things. It's too close to see. So it might reasonably take something as foreign to our experience as a medieval Italian poem, especially one as steeped in classical learning as this one, to focus some light on this blind spot. To see itself, the eye may need outside help.

Though I hope my personal respect for Christian thought and practice will be reflected throughout this book, classical involvements certainly helped bring me to Dante. In a sense, Virgil lighted the way. Like anyone who studies classical languages and literature at any length, I had fallen in love with some of the great pagan works and characters: Homer's poems, the Socrates in Plato's early dialogues, Sophocles' Theban plays, and eventually Virgil's *Aeneid*. Whatever their other virtues, works like these command admiration because they invigorate the mind. They raise new and unsettling questions that can't be easily dealt in familiar terms. For a literature teacher, that's one of the greatest of assets.

Dante got into the head of a secularist like me through a literary question that had come to have political implications: how would classically educated Christians in other ages have come to terms with the old pagan worthies? This question lands you right on the *Commedia*'s threshold, most emphatically because it highlights one of the poem's fundamental tensions. Here was a great piece of literature, written by a Christian who had avidly buried himself in what classical materials were available to him (plentiful Latin manuscripts but only those Greek texts that had been translated into Latin). Dante's learned piety promised to give me just what I was seeking: an authoritative Christian perspective on pagan thought at some distance from contemporary Christianity. In this, his *Commedia* was hardly disappointing. I found that the poem could be read as a series of attempts to show how the best of pagan thought can nourish a serious Christian's intellect and spirit.

Virgil was Dante's main course. As the first two-thirds of the *Commedia* make clear, Dante considers Virgil a superstar, arguably *the* superstar, of virtuous paganism. But since Dante couldn't have known very much about the historical figure, to him Virgil had to be primarily the author of the *Aeneid*. The scene in which Virgil first approaches the pilgrim (*Inferno* 1:64–87) bears this out. When Virgil reveals himself there to be the singer of the *Aeneid*, the pilgrim excitedly claims to have been a deep delver into that epic. His "long study" of this celebrated poem has elevated Virgil in his mind as teacher, stylistic model, and, the *Commedia* soon shows, paternal figure. (For the poet, the relationship is certainly more complex.) So any adequate answer to my virtuous-pagan question for the *Commedia* has to rise out of an understanding of Virgil and his *Aeneid*. What follows is my attempt to cover some of this ground.

Canto 1 of *Inferno* focuses attention on the pagans by raising one of the poem's richest and most fundamental questions: why would Dante choose Virgil, a pre-Christian Roman poet, as the pilgrim's initial guide to the Christian afterlife? It's the kind of open-ended question Dante loves, one that hovers above every canto of the *Inferno*. Your students can return to it beneficially again and again. Understanding what is known about the historical Virgil may help them somewhat. Through a little research, they might discover some interpretively useful similarities between Dante and Virgil as epic poets: both had achieved poetic renown before tackling the epic form; the epic masterpieces of both depended heavily on the influence and support of patrons; both epics had a lot of bearing on contemporary politics. And so on. Any good edition of the *Inferno* will provide your students with a little biographical knowledge about Virgil, but you would do well to supplement that. Perhaps the most authoritative source of short articles about classical matters is *The Oxford Classical Dictionary* (Hornblower, Spawforth, and Eidinow 2012). The Virgil entry there will provide you with a succinct and balanced discussion of what is known about the historical Virgil.

But that will only take you so far. Virgil's characterization in the *Commedia* has to carry most of the weight of Dante's assessment of him. That's something Dante develops over Virgil's entire sixty-four canto tenure in the poem, but your students can draw some provisional conclusions from passages in the poem's first cantos. Have them study closely the last half of canto 1, asking what kind of initial character the poet gives Virgil there. Encourage your students to visualize what is happening in this section in as much detail as the text will allow. Since this poem traffics so heavily in the tacit and the surreal, it richly rewards the play of visual imagination. Conjuring up the looks on Virgil's face as he deals with the hapless pilgrim is one of the pleasures of reading the *Inferno*. In the first pilgrim/Virgil meeting in canto 1, your students should see the principle of contrast strongly at work. Next to Virgil, the pilgrim should seem a weak, vacillating, fearful wretch, anxious to regain some positive sense of himself if only by association with someone better. So there is a kind of desperation in the way he fawns on Virgil. Much of Virgil's steady self-possession stands out in contrast to the pilgrim's timorousness. Right away, through what virtues Virgil exhibits here in calming and beginning to educate his pathetic charge, your students can begin to understand some of the strengths of virtuous paganism. Visual imagination helps because Virgil's characterization is often carried as much by what he doesn't do or say as what he does. In canto 1, the pilgrim's almost manic flattery, for example, evokes little response from Virgil in word or action. (What good is flattery to the damned?) Maybe we are to infer a mild rebuke: emotional restraint, not enthusiasm, should steer this Christian journey.

In analyzing Virgil's character, you may want to bring up the four cardinal classical virtues: prudence, justice, temperance, and fortitude. Dante refers to this list approvingly in several places in the *Commedia*. In fact, he organizes a big swath of *Paradiso* around this famous tetrad. Because these are the traditional measures of pagan greatness, we might expect Virgil to exhibit them. But they certainly won't exhaust his characterization, particularly since he becomes to the pilgrim not just a literary and moral mentor, but a revered father figure as well. You may find it hard to come to the end of the list of what Dante admires about Virgil.

Completing this list as sensitively as you can, though, will leave your ledger unbalanced. To a Christian poet, Virgil will have to exhibit limitations as well. He can't be the image of human perfection; else what would be the need for Christian revelation? In canto 4, Virgil describes the punishment of virtuous pagans like himself as "grief without torment" (4:28), expressed in the sighing the pilgrim hears in the surrounding air. The great pagans in limbo suffer not from some positive sin but from a lack of understanding of something to which they couldn't have had access: God's revelation of himself in Holy Scripture. Among other things, they miss the emphasis on Christian virtues like those listed by Paul: faith, hope, and love. The sighing of these pagans functions as an index of incompleteness: they long for something they can't comprehend. Trying to find the words to explain this lack might lead your students, as it did mine, into spirited conversation.

In addition to illustrating some of his virtues, then, you might expect canto 1 at least to hint at Virgil's shortcomings. At the end of the canto (1:124–29) Virgil uses the imagery of Roman political power to characterize God, whose dominance the pagans in limbo can feel but not fully understand. To Virgil, God is an emperor (*imperador*) on a high seat who doesn't just rule but exercises power (*impera*, not *regna*) over his city. A reflective Christian might feel that such imagery misses the mark. "Emperor" captures poorly the nature, position, and manner of acting of the Christian God. Virgil's use of this metaphor makes historical sense from someone who lived under Caesars, but applied to a Christian scheme it becomes a sign of Virgil's conceptual limitations. To Dante, virtuous paganism, however admirable, can't be enough. Throughout *Inferno*, Dante's Virgil will exhibit both worthiness and defect, often in the space of a few lines. Such complexity makes Virgil as guide an endlessly fertile literary device. It also expresses Dante's solution to a problem that preoccupies him: how to characterize the virtuous pagans? Tracing out Dante's protracted answer to this question in the *Inferno* can bring your students literary satisfactions of the highest order.

As Virgil, so the *Aeneid* (Lewis 1953). In a sense, the *Aeneid* raises the guide question but in a different domain: why does Dante model his Christian poem in so many ways on epic, a predominantly pagan genre? Starting with the poem's first line, he makes his debt apparent through frequent allusions to the conventions and formulae of classical epic. Dante begins his poem "mezzo"—in the middle—develops the first of many epic similes in his first canto, invokes the muse in canto 2, employs artificially long set speeches throughout the poem, adopts a lofty tone in a generally high linguistic register (though with much variation), gives prominent play to Aeneas and Odysseus and to a number of other figures from classical epic, frequently alludes to classical sources, builds his poem around the travails and triumphs of something like an epic hero, posits a world writ large encompassing something like the entirety of the Italian culture of his time, and has his protagonist work out his destiny within a divine superstructure that defines and complicates it. It would be hard to imagine a more blatant set of epic indicators, with numerous references to the *Aeneid* leaving by far the deepest classical footprint.

In effect, then, Dante announces an epic for Christians. By association, he means to ascribe to the *Commedia* epic weight, scope, and cultural authority. According to the Hollanders (*Inferno* 4:95–96n), Dante saw the epic form as a springboard to the loftiest poetic flights. Since Dante understood his poem to be dealing with the highest and most serious of human materials, what other established literary form would have done? Similarly for breadth. Epics evoke whole cultural worlds, like Mycenean Greece or post-republican Rome. Obviously Dante, too, aims for coverage. By that measure, you can hardly top a work that extends from Satan's ice to the Empyrean heavens. To someone with Dante's background, thinking of literary range means thinking of epic. The great sweep of traditional epics often corresponds to richness of cultural implication. Epic poems are culturally value-laden. Through the travails of their heroes, they paint a richly complex picture, expressing the struggles, values, and aspirations of an entire culture or nation at a given historical moment. Dante's *Commedia* offers to educated Italians in his day (and to a global audience since) a fully digested vision of God's complete creative enterprise, as the best philosophy and theology of his time would have understood it. For Dante, there could be no better poetic form in which to couch such a bold project.

This choice must have set him in complicated relation to the classical epic masters he admired so much. For his masterwork, simple reverent emulation clearly would not carry much weight. The complexity of such literary connections between great poets is the subject of a famous book by Harold Bloom (1997) called *The Anxiety of Influence.* Among the many contentions in that difficult work, Bloom develops the claim that a strong poet invariably works out his artistic destiny under the influence of one or more strong predecessors. The result is creative anxiety in the successor poet, perhaps similar to that felt by, say, Peyton Manning before he took his first snap or maybe George W. Bush before his first campaign speech. To derive as ingeniously as possible or to originate? Strong young poets like Dante have to learn to manage such conflicting impulses. The result, according to Bloom, can be great literature in a new generation. In his dealings with Virgil, the *Aeneid*, and the epic form generally, you can feel Dante working through something like the push and pull of this conflict.

The push would result partly from Dante's personal relationship with the epic muse and partly from the force of the "Christian" in Christian epic. You'll have to pick up a sense of the former as you go, but the latter can be a matter of discussion for your students from the beginning. What specific features of form or approach, and not just subject matter, distinguish Dante's poem from its classical forebears? You could start by asking your students how classical epic qualities like weight, size, and cultural authority work differently in a Christian context. The *Commedia* is indeed weighty, but not from the glorious activities of elite aristocratic warriors who fight in the front. Instead, its heft rests on that "our" in its first line and on its depiction of the struggles of an everyman to understand his moral and spiritual position in the divine scheme. Spatially, Dante needs to display the structure of the entire created universe to demonstrate some features about God's creation that would be beyond any classical understanding of the divine. As the inscription over the gates of hell in canto 3 suggests, Dante sees the universe as evidence of God's intelligence, justice, and love. It makes sense, is morally binding, and reflects benign intent. None of these unqualified claims can be made about the cosmos implied in the *Aeneid*, much less the *Odyssey* or *Iliad*.

Your best vehicle for examining both sides of Dante's relation to Virgil and the *Aeneid* might be a comparison of the epic heroes of the *Aeneid* and the *Commedia*. Dante the poet invites this comparison in canto 2 through some apprehensive, perhaps even cowardly, comments the pilgrim makes. In response to Virgil's urging him forward toward the necessary "arduous passage," the pilgrim cowers. Stacking himself up unfavorably against Aeneas and Paul, two previous living journeyers into the underworld, the pilgrim doubts his own ability to make the trip:

> But why should I go there? Who allows it?
> I am not Aeneas, nor am I Paul.
> Neither I nor any think me fit for this.
>
> And so, if I commit myself to come,
> I fear it may be madness. You are wise,
> You understand what I cannot express. (2:31–36)

As commentators have pointed out, these lines can be read ironically at the pilgrim's expense. In fact he is similar in significant ways to both predecessors, but especially to Aeneas. It will be helpful here to line up in your students' minds the protagonists of the great classical epics. Dante the pilgrim has much more in common with Aeneas, and vice-versa, than with Achilles or Odysseus. The two Homeric heroes, whatever external obstacles they face, remain supremely confident in their own powers and in their sense of position or direction. Achilles always knows he is the best of the Greek fighters, destined to achieve undying glory on the battlefield at Troy. Odysseus suffers many losses but seldom questions his crafty ability to turn circumstances to his advantage. Aside from a dalliance or two, he keeps his head turned toward Ithaka with great determination.

Initially, Aeneas has more of the psychology of a loser. He is, after all, a Trojan who barely escaped his burning city with most of his family, some supporters, and a few ships. Early in Virgil's poem he seems not much more than a homeless wanderer, with little sense of definite direction. Virgil convincingly develops in him the distraught, disoriented mind of a warrior who has seen his entire culture destroyed in a ten-year war. What ultimately guides him is *pietas*, his defining virtue and the quality of character that Virgil most wants to celebrate as supremely Roman. Pietas in Virgil's sense is broader than Christian piety because it includes reverence to nation and family in addition to the divine. But it is a lot closer to a Christian's sense of worthy character than is Homeric emotional/physical power or resourceful cleverness of mind. As Aeneas moves around the Mediterranean, he begins to understand his mission and to grow into his role, particularly after visiting the underworld and hearing his father read him his future. After that scene in the middle of the *Aeneid*, Aeneas becomes more an instrument of Roman destiny than an individual with his own needs and agendas. This image of an individual called to sacrifice himself in the service of a greater good should also resonate with Christians. With some help from you, your students will begin to understand how Aeneas might be called a post-Greek and a pre-Christian hero. (Virgil has for millennia, in fact, been celebrated as the most Christian of classical poets. Some have thought that his *Fourth Eclogue* predicts the coming of Christ.) They might begin to see how, at least in initial psychology and situation, the pilgrim in a dark wood, lost almost beyond any helping, is not unlike Aeneas. This Virgilian hero pulls pretty strongly at Dante's imagination.

In general, Dante does not want to simply reject the precursor cultures that have played prominent roles in the development and ultimate dominance of Catholic Christianity in Italy. This stands to reason. To steal a line from Flannery O'Connor's (1986) *Wise Blood*, God's creation might be seen as a "vast construction work that involved the whole order of the universe and would take all time to complete" (18). Then God is a master builder, with natural and human history his ongoing projects. If so, Greek, and especially Roman, culture would constitute some of his essential building materials, contributing necessarily to effects visible in Dante's own time. This idea of intelligible, inclusive order permeates the *Commedia* and is essential to Dante's thinking about how God works in time. To Dante, God would not give humans the power of reason for it to languish in an absurd universe fundamentally alien to it.

But in the depiction of heroes, Dante the poet ultimately pushes back. The pilgrim is a Christian protagonist without the pre-, and that has to matter. In the pilgrim's story, the task is ultimately individual salvation, not cultural destiny. Being lost is primarily a spiritual condition, not a historical one. To find his way, one character has to overcome external obstacles to visit an underworld where he will learn from his father what course he must take to gain a foothold in Italy, while the other has to overcome fear so as to get an education into what human souls can become anywhere, based on their choices. The autumn leaves simile in canto 3 (112–20) has sometimes been cited to sharpen this distinction. This simile alludes to a similar one in book 6 of the *Aeneid* (6:309–12). Both passages compare souls massing to cross the Acheron into the underworld in Charon's boat to falling leaves. But while Virgil deals with his souls in the plural through generations of leaves, Dante individualizes his. Twice Dante mentions how the souls of the damned fall into Charon's boat, as leaves fall from a bough, one at a time. This emphasis on individuality seems distinctively Christian. Virgil's protagonist, Aeneas, is a fundamentally Roman hero, not an everyman. He learns to count the leaves in generations. But where Aeneas needs to suppress his personal intentions in the name of his service to a future Rome, Dante the pilgrim has to come to individual terms with God. In that sense, to a Christian poet, the pilgrim's journey can be *ours*.

You can make a similar point here using Beatrice, which presents you with a good opportunity to focus some attention on her. Though she appears only indirectly in *Inferno*, as in this canto where Virgil recounts a conversation with her, understanding Beatrice is essential to understanding Dante's poem and, from what we can gather from his earlier work, his life. Later in the poem she figures prominently: in canto 30 of *Purgatorio*, she takes over from Virgil as the pilgrim's guide and proceeds to usher him from there up through most of *Paradiso*. Historically, as any edition of *Inferno* will tell you, Beatrice Portinari was a Florentine woman with whom Dante as a young man fell platonically in love. When she died in 1290 in her mid-twenties, a grieving Dante was apparently left with the rest of his life to work out what she meant to him. According to Dorothy Sayers (1950), she became for Dante "that person . . . [whom] by arousing his adoring love, has become for him the God-bearing image, the revelation of the presence of God" (67). In the present canto we learn that she has descended from heaven to intercede with Virgil on the pilgrim's behalf in the hope of rescuing him from the dark wood. Without divine intervention through her, we are to understand, the pilgrim would have been lost.

Even with the help of Sayers and other commentators, I find the meaning of Beatrice in this poem elusive. But one idea seems clear enough: she is positioned here in canto 2 as a personal conduit of divine concern for Dante Alighieri, the specific individual. Her role in the poem is to help carry out a divine rescue plan for the soul of Dante the pilgrim. For other pilgrims, presumably, the Virgin Mary would have sent other rescuers. The analogous figure in the *Aeneid* is again Aeneas' father Anchises. In his meeting with his son in the underworld, Anchises likewise couches Aeneas' future in the framework of a plan. But his focus is on the founding of Rome, not on the inner life of Aeneas the individual. The Beatrice/Anchises contrast points up again a fundamental difference in focus between Christian and classical Roman thought, as least as Dante would see it. Though there is much more to be said about the role of Beatrice in the poem, this comparison may give you a start. Your Christian students should have a lot to say about what distinguishes this pilgrim's situation from that of his epic forebears.

Such considerations as these, and others you may come to from a little *Aeneid* research, can enrich your students' study of *Inferno* all along the way, since the guide/pilgrim relationship develops prominently throughout the poem. The inexhaustibility of investigations like these is one clear sign of the *Commedia*'s worth, as I hope your students will begin to understand.

In his handling of the pagans, Dante takes steps in what I want to call an ecumenical direction. His God has dispensed some light to all his human creatures. That conception has the power to bridge a lot of the crevasses that fracture the current political, cultural, and religious landscape. To me, that makes Dante an indispensable Christian writer for the contemporary literature classroom. He'll involve your students in what literature can do very well: foster conversation toward a better understanding of what divides them from others.

Exercises

CLOSE READING

1. You can hardly spend too much time with your students unpacking a great writer's figures of speech. Besides being critical to understanding the poem, Dante's richly suggestive similes and allusions will develop interpretive muscle in your students. Have them try the simile at 2: 127f. The poet compares the pilgrim's resurgent courage for the journey to flowers, closed at night, that open when they feel the sun's rays. Thinking through the implications of the flower imagery here might prompt some of your students to detect some irony. The pilgrim's moods seem a bit mercurial, vacillating like the opening and closing of a flower's petals according to changing conditions. How is Virgil characterized here? Have your students try to see the look on the face of the head whose back the excitable pilgrim sees as they move ahead. What should they make of Virgil's silence here?

2. Under the emphasis on Dante's classical education and pagan influences, you could set up the close examination of an allusion to the *Aeneid*. The leaf similes at *Aeneid* 6:309–14 and *Inferno* 3:112–20 will certainly do. With allusions, as with similes and metaphors, your questions should be comparative. How would knowledge of the vehicle, Virgil's passage, enrich your understanding of the tenor, Dante's characterization of the souls about to cross the river Acheron into hell? Parallels, contrasts, or some combination of the two might govern your students' interpretive comments. Good figures of speech, especially Dante's, invite a variety of interpretive responses. Which is not to say that anything ought to go. You should be as ready to challenge readings that contradict the text as to stand corrected in light of what a student claims. When warranted, though, the latter reaction can do more for the health of your classroom than any other gesture you can make. It's worth repeating that Singleton's (1990) commentary will be your

most thorough source for identifying allusions to the *Aeneid* and other works throughout *Inferno*. Shorter editions offer some help as well.

3. On Virgil's characterization as an expression of Dante's view of the greatest pagans, you could have your students look in the first two cantos at how Virgil's speech reveals the kind of character Dante gives him. His virtues, especially when contrasted with the flaws in the wretched pilgrim, should shine. But since to a Christian even the best of the pagans has to fall short, make sure to have your students analyze the language Virgil uses to describe (at 2:124–29) the God he cannot know. These lines, perhaps, begin to balance the scale by suggesting areas where Virgil's worldly wisdom is limited. An Italian dictionary might help you here by suggesting other words Virgil could have used to characterize divine authority. You might also have them consider, as a preface to canto 4, the puzzling word *ribellante* that Virgil uses to describe his relation to God (1:125). In what sense can "rebelled" characterize the relation of early Greeks or Romans to the God they could not have known? Perhaps this would be the place to raise the question of Virgil's allegorical function in the poem. (See Themes and Issues, 2 below.)

4. You might have your students consider the first six lines of canto 2, one of my favorite passages in the poem. I'm betting you have seen commencement passages like this one in other literature. The point, I think, is to contrast "creatures of the earth" that live by natural cycles with human beings, for whom life is not that simple or contented. So what is it about human beings that distinguishes us from animals as suggested by the pilgrim's need to take this difficult journey?

THEMES AND ISSUES

1. Pilgrim versus poet: your students should see the beginning of *Inferno* as choreographing maximum distance between the pilgrim, who Beatrice tells Virgil is almost beyond saving, and the poet, who has made the journey to heaven, seen the divine light, and returned with a commission to encompass the entire picture in a work of art. Where in the first two cantos do we see this distancing? You can often identify it from the sense of irony you feel when the pilgrim does or says something over which we feel the poet/ narrator shaking his head. Of course, ironic undermining, often subtle in this poem, lies somewhat in the eyes of the beholder. Still, since the poet doesn't often criticize the spineless pilgrim directly, there must logically be places, probably of diminishing force as the poem proceeds, where the poet implicitly communicates the pilgrim's lack of maturity and understanding. Where do we see this in the first two cantos?

2. Ultimately, your Virgil discussions over the first two cantos might rise to a consideration of his allegorical function in the poem. If you follow the suggestion that the poem can be seen allegorically as describing the landscape of the human soul, then Virgil, too, should be taken to represent some inner tendency or possibility. But you should encourage your students to be dubious about any claim that neatly washes out Virgil's individuality in favor of some abstraction. Help them keep some critical distance from formulae like Ciardi's notion that Virgil equals human reason. Dante is no reductionist. His great trick is somehow to impart representative power to people and their actions without losing the distinctiveness of the individual human being. Dante's Virgil has first and mainly to be the poet who lived and worked in Rome during the reign of Augustus Caesar. And "human reason" seems inadequate to many of the features of the human soul that Virgil can be taken to embody. What we are to admire seems so much more than just his power to reason.

    One possible take: As the pilgrim's struggles to come to better terms with God's elaborately constructed moral and spiritual order can be seen as every soul's struggle, so Virgil can seem to represent the natural man at his best, short of access to Christian revelation. Allegorized, then, Virgil would be the best shape that a human soul can take based entirely on the development of the whole range of faculties natural to human beings. As the poem makes abundantly clear, that, to Dante, is a lot. It might define the perfect guide through a place illustrating how those powers can be abused or perverted.

Research

1. Here I want to cite generally an obvious area of research for this chapter's topic: Dante and the pagans. Your students could study to great profit any of the elements of Dante's poetic lineage. Though I'll develop this idea more completely later, I'll mention here the main line of heroes: first Odysseus and Achilles, who influenced so strongly Virgil's thinking about character in the *Aeneid*, then Aeneas, who served the same function for Dante. Because an epic hero is by definition emblematic of the values of a culture or people, tracing the progression of these heroes arguably gets you to essentials about how these cultures understood themselves. This can be an education in itself. Have your students read up on the characterizations of these heroes under the push and pull question for Dante. What features of classical heroes does Dante want to re-create; how does he want to distinguish his pilgrim from previous epic protagonists? A more challenging

version of this project would involve asking the same sorts of questions for whole poems. To respond to that, a student would have to read the Homeric and Virgilian epics with comparative questions in mind. That's a time-consuming task, but rich beyond imagining for that student who is serious about understanding the foundations of his own culture. The questions after chapter 7 will develop this line of questioning more thoroughly.

2. More modestly, you could have students find a reputable brief discussion of epic as a form to be used as a basis for a more thoughtful answer to the question of why Dante wanted to clothe his poem in epic trappings. (Again, see chapter 7's questions.)

Extension

1. One sign of an old piece of literature's vitality lies in how readily its ideas can be extended into other places and times. As that "our" in the first line implies, Dante means to ace this test. In the *Commedia*, after all, God has structured his universe to last for all time. If so, dependable guides might always be indispensable. So have your students take personally the matter of guides. Keeping all that Virgil is to Dante in mind, your students might consider as deeply as possible whom God would send them as a guide through the challenging moral terrain through which all humans must make their way. Each student could work up her response to this question in writing or as a presentation to class. Require her to defend her choice with frequent references to Virgil. You might let this project develop slowly over a complete reading of the *Inferno*, so that Virgil's full weight has been felt. Alternatively, your class as a whole could work on the question of an appropriate national guide for Americans in this age, and so on.

2. Or you could also have them work on literary influence, analogous to Virgil's on Dante. They could read up on acknowledged poetic influences of some poet of their choice. Choosing one particular influential predecessor, they would try to determine the exact nature of his influence and how the chosen poet responded to that influence. The results could be presented in the form of a discussion of two poems, one from the predecessor and one from the poet, carefully chosen to illustrate quite specifically the nature of literary influence in this case. This exercise is not as daunting as it may sound: some of my students made good use of it.

3

Contrapasso

CANTOS 4 AND 5

Christian theology sometimes troubles me, particularly some of the popular versions of God's scheme of rewards and punishments. I think that puts me in company with not just skeptics and secularists but some Christian theologians. My objection goes like this: why would God, the source of a highly intelligible universe, create a scheme in which human choices and their divinely ordained consequences are so discontinuous? God punishes the temporal sin I commit today in an atemporal realm completely separate from this one and in a manner reflecting the sin faintly, if at all. In this world, my sins *need* not have any detrimental effect upon my state of being, but in the next life, if I die unrepentant, God will punish my sins eternally in a form appropriate in at most one dimension, their gravity. Under this view, when it comes to moral cause and effect, this world and the next seem pretty thinly correlated.

Such a perspective would encourage believers to think prudentially. Since moral rewards and punishments aren't very reliable in this world, you do good and avoid evil to acquire a happy placement in the eternal hereafter. As Pascal pointed out in his wager, this just makes good sense. Believers in this logic can see situations in this world as little more than instruments to be manipulated in the service of prudent self-interest. I realize this is hardly a complete account of the range of Christian teaching on this matter. But experience tells me it is the view of many avowed Christians, a good number of my students among them. And probably always has been.

I can't see how the Christian God would endorse such a perspective—how rational self-interest as the foundation of moral thought and action can be made compatible with God's intentions as depicted in the Bible. I have to assume that the perspective (or my framing of it) is distorted or incomplete. What picture would accord more closely with the biblical God's image? Perhaps one in which there are some stronger this-worldly reasons to avoid sin. Strip away other-worldly arguments and the problem is similar to the one Socrates's two young interlocutors put to him early in Plato's *Republic*. Roughly: "Tell us, Socrates, why one should act justly, irrespective of worldly rewards and punishments, which, as everyone knows, may not have much to do with justice? Why does it make sense to do good in difficult or painful situations even when no one is watching?" (See Lee 2003, *Republic* Book 2: 357a–367e.)

As I read him, Dante has an answer to such questions. For punishments, Dante develops that answer throughout *Inferno*. His name for it is the *contrapasso*. This is the term Dante uses to define the relationship in God's divine scheme between what humans do and what they experience as a result. In *Inferno*, the contrapasso connects sins with their commensurate consequences. The root *-passo* comes from the Greek verb *pasko*, which means "to suffer" in the sense of "to be acted upon." So etymologically, *contrapasso* would mean something like counterexperience: that is, what someone has to experience in response to what he chooses to do. Dante uses the term only once in the entire *Inferno*, but in a way that invites application in every circle. It is spoken in canto 28 by Bertrand de Born, a promoter of schisms who aptly carries his head in his hand. From that severed head he proclaims, "Thus the contrapasso observes itself in me." Here Dante gives a name to one of *Inferno*'s most profound interpretive problems: what exactly is the relation between what the various sinners have chosen to do in the world above and what they are suffering below?

Whatever their religious affiliations, your students might find Dante's answer worth pondering. Cantos 4 and 5 provide a good start toward understanding that answer. Consider the virtuous pagans in *Inferno* 4, the first circle of hell: Limbo. The individual shades dwelling there include some of history's most noteworthy figures, the cream of classical antiquity: Socrates, Plato, Aristotle, Homer, Virgil himself, and others. Dante has brazenly located these pagan greats, who lived before the time of Christ, in hell. Call this justice?

When you look closely at it, though, the pagans' contrapasso in canto 4 doesn't seem much like punishment. The sounds of suffering here are muted: sighs instead of lamentations. Here a benign "blaze of light that overcame a hemisphere of darkness" (4:68–69) relieves the pervasive murkiness of hell. Since they lived before Christ, even the best of the pagans did not know how to worship God adequately. For this reason alone, Virgil explains, "without hope we live on in longing" (4:42). Pagan suffering in hell is thus based not on acts of commission but on an inadvertent omission. Though the figures in this first circle did not sin, their words and actions here reflect an awareness of some very important matter to which even the most brilliant among them were denied access. Otherwise, Limbo looks fairly appealing. The great pagans spend eternity doing pretty much what pagan intellectuals were supposed to like to do: stroll about in an Arcadian landscape in conversation with other celebrated philosophers and poets. That seems less like punishment than the fulfillment of a pagan's dream. In fact, the situation in this canto closely reflects Socrates's vision in Plato's *Apology* (Tarrant 2003) of what death may entail. The thought of hemlock doesn't faze him much because of what dying may lead to: an afterlife of good conversation with the best of previous pagan thinkers.

It would be a mistake, though, to conclude that there is no real suffering in this circle. The canto's language won't support that reading. The souls in Limbo feel "anguish" and "grief" because they are "lost" and "without hope." Virgil, Limbo-dweller himself when not out guiding, turns pale out of pity for the pain here. But this suffering is appropriately located in the mind, not the body. The virtuous pagans now seem to comprehend how inescapably limited had been their earthly understanding. Through no fault of their own, their vision had been too narrow. To an intellectual on the level of an Aristotle or Plato, realizing that would hurt.

But in the context of the *Commedia*, this pain is not illogical. If you make the Christian revelation vital to the soul's well-being, then its absence has to matter decisively. So the virtuous pagans sigh in realization of and hopeless longing for the knowledge they lacked. Sin corresponds so closely to punishment here that it is hard to call the result punishment. Take Virgil's mind at death, give it a visible form, add his disturbing realization that his earthly understanding was limited, and you have the essence of the first circle. To your more reflective students, the pagans' position in limbo might seem like the eternal reflection of the life they chose to live above.

You can make the same case in canto 5, one of the most celebrated in *Inferno*. It features the shade of Francesca da Rimini, who acts as an embodiment of lust. Lines 28 to 51 comprise the general contrapasso of those whose lives were governed by the desire for erotic pleasure. Ask your students to use their imagination on these lines. Have them try to express in their own images the inner condition of people who have made sexual desire the law of their being. (Such exercises may make them uncomfortable, but that, after all, is the point. In *Inferno*, Dante is not out to comfort anyone. I hope you see that as a virtue.) Being driven uncontrollably by a haphazard but powerful wind might approximate pretty closely what they come up with. Under the question of how suffering is appropriate to sin here, work through these lines in detail with them. Don't let them neglect the two bird similes. It should all cohere in a picture of a particular human capacity gone awry.

But Dante doesn't leave things there. To the general imagery of the contrapasso of lust, canto 5 adds the first case of a device that is an *Inferno* essential:

a conversation between a sinner and Dante/Virgil in which the sinner reveals who he or she is without intending to. Through the pilgrim's encounter with Francesca, Dante the poet very alluringly individualizes his picture of lust. Many a reader, including some famous ones, has fallen for the image of Francesca presented here. It has proved hard not to follow the pilgrim in some kind of swoon by the end of this canto. Which only makes sense, so powerfully seductive is the force she embodies.

There is a deeper logic to Francesca's allure based in Dante's allegorical method. If Francesca were no more than the personified abstraction of lust, she would be easy to condemn. But Dante doesn't work that way. He's interested in the idea of lust lodged in a particular human soul. A sin humanized means a sin complicated by all the other features that contribute to a human personality. It is hard not to find yourself sympathizing with some elements of any person you get to know pretty well, let alone someone like Francesca, no matter how repugnant she might seem on a first take. In Dante's hands, allegory can be at once representative and individual. The tension between these two dimensions constitutes one of the poem's great beauties. Once identified, it is almost guaranteed to generate some good classroom discussion.

Having logged countless screen hours, your students should find the Francesca trope familiar. She's the woman who can flatter and flirt her way to what she wants from men. Movies abound in images of this woman-as-temptress kind. But Dante makes his developed characters hard to pigeonhole, Francesca particularly. Her appeal rests on much more than physical allure. She's more like an Anna Karenina than, say, a Marilyn Monroe. Questions like the following might help your students avoid any quick jump into stereotype:

1. What is Francesca trying to accomplish in her brief conversation with Dante (5:89f)?
2. What devices or strategies does she use to achieve her desired effects? What accounts for her appeal to men inside and outside the poem? Do the young women in your classroom react to her differently than the guys?
3. How does Dante the poet structure the scene to reveal more about her than she intends? In other words, where are there ironic signals that run counter to her intentions?
4. How then does the poet intend for his readers to respond to Francesca?

From her first few lines, Francesca flirtatiously attempts to stir up sympathy and maybe something more in the minds of her two male visitors, the pilgrim and his guide. She will have more success with one than the other, as she seems to know, since she addresses herself mainly to the pilgrim. Have your students study closely the devices she uses and the effects she hopes to achieve by them. Thus Dante gives a human form to lust. She flatters unctuously, projects a dubious prayerful piety and employs softly alluring language to attain her aims. But the canto's tour de force occurs at lines 100–108 in the love poem she recites to deny her culpability. Notice how through strong verbs (seized, seized, brought us) she casts Amor as a kind of personified force whom one is powerless to resist. To her, even in hell, Love is a god (versus Christianity's God is love?). How can she and Paolo be faulted for yielding to him? She uses a similarly literary strategy in her description of their fateful dalliance. The book was to blame. Your students probably know enough about the Arthurian legends to evaluate this claim. Have them think of the Lancelot/Guinevere consummation in its Arthurian context. What kind of reader infers sexual permission from the event in that story that eventually destroys Camelot? Obviously, one who knows what she is looking for and who has already convinced herself not to think much beyond the boundaries of a longed-for moment. How much daylight do you see between that Francesca and this one, between the woman above and the shade below?

The story of Francesca's fall as she spins it out (5:89f) sweeps Dante the pilgrim away. Does the poet want her to have the same effect on his audience? Or is this a place where your students are supposed to sense ironic distance between pilgrim and poet? These thorny interpretive issues confront readers in this and a few other famous *Inferno* cantos, the ones he builds around characters who seem, at first blush, sympathetic. Those cantos will puzzle your students by raising the "Should the damned be pitied?" question in the poem's most ambiguous situations. Take that puzzlement to be beneficial.

"What I was alive, I am in death" (14:51). So admits Capaneus the blasphemer in canto 14, in a statement that echoes throughout *Inferno*. The surprisingly close relation between bad behavior in life and punishment in death sets Dante's Christian vision apart from any other I've seen. I think this proximity holds true throughout *Inferno*, though admittedly in some places the case is harder to make than in cantos 4 and 5. Literary duty obliges you to draw out with your students the implications of this distinctive, and I think profound, causal pattern. It is open to many possible interpretations, which should encourage you in working out your own. I read the text as inducing readers to see punishments in *Inferno* as continuations of the lives that sinners chose to live above. Through the choices they make on earth, people gradually fashion a soul that will become externally visible in the afterlife. Death is not so much a barrier as a permeable membrane through which the essence of the soul constructed in life freely passes. To use the classical medical metaphor for lack of proper care for the soul, God lands each diseased soul in external conditions in hell reflective of what that soul has made of itself. By placement in an appropriate circle, God adds to individual portraits of the damned details characterizing their type. What the historical Francesca shares with the lustful element in any soul is vulnerability to the winds of sexual passion. You could describe the pilgrim's entire journey through the *Commedia* as an education in the proper response to the self-portrait each soul has painted (with God doing some touching up). Literally he's Dante Alighieri in 1300, allegorically he's every soul coming to understand the elements of its own nature anytime. I see the *Commedia* as supporting such a reading at many points, though it of course admits other interpretations as well. The approach I favor has one strong advantage: it has Dante providing you and your students with a provocative way to identify sinful behavior: it is any choice one carries out that damages, or sickens, the soul. Therefore, while alive you will naturally want to act so as to keep your soul healthy, and if you wake up one day with a soul lost in darkness, you'll hasten to seek out curative medicine.

I don't claim originality for this line of interpretation, though some of its conclusions I have not seen drawn before. It appeals to me because it provides a this-worldly rationale for living a good life: avoid sin because it damages your soul. Even my least-religious students have found this logic worth thinking about because it gives them earthly reasons for choosing to live a good life. And I don't see why Christians should find this position objectionable. It doesn't challenge any significant element of orthodox Christian belief but rather fills a theological gap. In doing so, it makes God the author of a more intelligible moral universe. This approach became my primary means for pulling students into this poem. It established a basis for conversation across the classroom. The importance of that will be my excuse for bringing it up repeatedly in later chapters.

All my inferences about the contrapasso are of course debatable. You can certainly read *Inferno* fruitfully without them. But I doubt that you can read it at any depth without coming to terms with the relations between sin and consequence it lays out so provocatively. As far as I know, the insistence on the intimacy of that relation is unique to Dante. God's moral logic, as Dante understands it, is configured there.

Exercises

CLOSE READING

1. The contrapasso question: In any circle of hell it makes sense to ask your students about the appropriateness of a punishment given the type of sin situated there. Answering this question requires careful reading of those

parts of the text that offer generic descriptions of a circle's sufferings. The trick is to get the details to cohere in a picture that renders intelligible God's scheme of moral cause and effect. Cantos 4 and 5 are good places to begin establishing a mode of inquiry that should become habitual to your students as they follow the journey through *Inferno*. (For canto 4, lines 25–42 or so; for canto 5, lines 28–49.)

2. Dante packs canto 5 more densely than usual with epic similes, three times comparing the lustful to birds. He likens the collective movements of these shades to that of flocks of starlings (40–42) and of lines of cranes (46–48). Then he compares Francesca and Paolo separately to a pair of mating doves (82–87). Spending time unpacking Dante's similes is always rewarding, but it seems almost necessary here where he makes such concentrated use of this device.

3. As outlined above, investigate what specific strategies Francesca uses, beginning at line 88, to appeal to the journeyers, what motivates her to use them, and how convincing they are. This is ultimately a question about tone. What attitude toward this character does the poet want his readers to share and how does he manage to convey that through Francesca's speech?

4. The Hollanders' notes put emphasis on the importance of repeated words in a given canto. For canto 4, they identify the dominant word as "honor," which occurs seven times during lines 72–100 (*Inferno* 4:72n). For *Inferno* 5, they highlight eleven occurrences of "love" and four of "pity" (5:91–93n). Among other things, such repetitions suggest that Dante holds cantos pretty discrete conceptually. In a given canto, repeated language alerts us to some motif or issue specific to that canto.

    a. For canto 4 you might point out that in the pagan world honor has often gone down as the most precious of human attainments. Homeric heroes like Achilles care for nothing more than their personal honor. This leads to problems, particularly in the *Iliad*. In the *Aeneid*, however, *pietas* (or reverence for parents, country and the gods) ultimately displaces honor as chief among Roman values, at least in literature. Western history in general might be said to chronicle the gradual unseating of honor from its pagan throne.

    The emphasis on honor in this canto generates questions that are, again, fundamentally comparative. In a Christian context, should a careful reader construe this pagan penchant for personal honor as a virtue or a shortcoming? How compatible is honor with essential Christian virtues like faith, hope, and love? Questions like this again demand some subtlety in responding to tone. If your students think that Dante intends to question the ultimate value of honor, make them point to specific word choices, images, or syntactical devices by which Dante communicates his doubts.

b. Linked together, love and pity, the two repeated words in canto 5, raise a question fundamental to *Inferno* regarding the proper response to the damned. In the scene itself, we have two models from which to construct an answer. All Francesca's talk about "Amor" so strongly affects the pilgrim that she overcomes him with pity (5:71), draws him so far into her sphere that he begins imitating her poeticized speech (112–20), and finally leaves him overcome in an emotion-driven swoon. That's a pretty sympathetic set of reactions. Meanwhile, what's his guide doing? Dante entirely conceals Virgil's response to Francesca so that it has to be inferred from his characterization in previous cantos. He certainly does not swoon. Your students may sense a contrast in reactions here, and supported by what Francesca reveals about herself, be moved to see some ironic distance between poet and pilgrim. Having made the entire journey, the poet may not consider swooning an adequate response to Francesca's carnality. However they come down on this interpretive problem, your students will be tackling one of most humanly and theologically profound of *Inferno* questions: should the damned be pitied? If not, what response would the poet endorse? Suggest that they respond to this as precisely as possible.

THEMES AND ISSUES

1. The vexing (and potentially inflammatory) question of God's justice should be addressed. Does this poem convincingly justify the ways of the Christian God to readers who take it seriously? Given the lives they lived, can the punishment of Paolo and Francesca be called just? Ditto for those of Virgil, Socrates, and the other pagans, who are sentenced to Limbo for a shortcoming that their place in history wouldn't allow them to avoid? I think you will find that this question can fuel almost endless debate among your interested students (and some of the less interested ones might find themselves leaning in).

Obviously, it is premised on general agreement about how the contrapasso works in these cantos. You may have to postulate that at the start, or classroom comments will spin off hotly in disconnected directions. And since questions like this can edge in pretty close to cherished beliefs, you will do well to mark off the playing field as exactly as possible. You may have to remind your students pretty forcefully that this is a question about Dante, about his presentation of God's moral scheme. For the sake of keeping the discussion inclusive, I think you should encourage your students to try to make arguments that don't completely rely on premises that their classmates can't share. That should hold personal testimonials of faith, however well concealed, to a minimum. The point of course is to be faithful to Dante and to reasonable notions of justice. Such restrictions shouldn't prove too restrictive. Your students will still find plenty of territory worth defending. Don't let them shy away from the eternity of the punishments in *Inferno*. That may be the hardest infernal morsel to swallow, but no defender of Dante's views can afford to ignore it.

You should include some treatment of the allegorical dimension: virtuous paganism is a faculty or potential in the human soul, in this case the optimal development of powers natural to human beings. In dealing with *Inferno* 4, link Virgil to anyone's natural self in its most complete, balanced, and reflective form, something close to the humanistic vision of the best human life. How are they to evaluate Dante's limbo picture of the ultimate consequences of this humanistic choice at its best? Can they see divine justice operating here?

For canto 5, reading allegorically may simplify the matter of what response to take to God's handling of someone like Francesca. Francesca and her like represent the sexual drive that is a biological dimension of all humans, one that contemporary culture shamelessly exploits. Allegory should push your students toward taking this matter personally. Canto 5 pictures the consequences of answering the carnal call with an unqualified yes. Are such consequences just?

2.   What is the relation between pilgrim and poet in canto 4 when the pilgrim takes pride in walking together with the great poets of antiquity? In canto 5 when the pilgrim swoons out of sympathy with Francesca?

3.   Canto 5 is one of the most literary of *Inferno*'s cantos. It contains a piece of troubadour love poetry, a critical reference to a book about Camelot, a likely allusion to Augustine's *Confessions* (see Research 2 below), and even cranes who fly in a line chanting poetic songs as they go. The close relation between literature and love (or lust) would seem to be thematically central to this canto. What does Dante want to communicate through that relationship? Good answers to this question might require knowledge of literary history that your students are unlikely to have. But you could prime them with an analogous contemporary query: in what ways are their own notions of romantic love conditioned by the films and television programs they have consumed?

Research

1.   Cantos 4 and 5 provide particularly rich possibilities for research. You can use any of the projects outlined below to generate written work, material for class presentation or both. For virtuous paganism in canto 4, I would highly recommend that you have your whole class put aside Dante for a day or two to read Plato's *Apology* (Tarrant 2003). Written by an eye-witness, it purports to be a dramatized rendition of the defense speech Socrates gave at his trial for disregarding the gods and corrupting the youth of Athens. Its brevity (thirty to forty pages) and accessibility make it the best primary entry into the "noble castle" of classical paganism. You could also have your students read the last few pages of Plato's *Phaedo*, which recount Socrates' death scene. Nothing I know of could better prepare your students for a savvy reading of *Inferno* 4 than this material. Here is virtuous paganism at its most memorable. What do they think of Dante's Christian handling of it?

   If you don't take up the *Apology* here, I fervently hope you find some place in your course for it. Though the Socrates pictured there can spawn heated debate in several directions, there is no more renowned defense of the life of rational investigation than this. Try not to let this exercise become antiquarian. If we believe cultural historians, Socrates and the other great pagans still live in Western minds. Their tradition is fundamental to who we are.

2.   Take a similar approach to Augustine in canto 5. Some scholars believe that Francesca's most suggestive line—"That day we read in it no further." (5:138)—is an allusion to one of the greatest non-biblical Christian events in history: the conversion of Saint Augustine. If so, the line refers to the climactic moment in Augustine's *Confessions* (Chadwick 2009), an autobiographical work that chronicles the saint's progress from dissolute youth through an attraction to various forms of pagan philosophical learning to a sudden and unexpected conversion to Christianity. In book 8 of *Confessions*, Augustine reconstructs in dramatic detail the scene of his conversion. He couches the decisive moment in language very close to Francesca's fateful line (See book 8, chapter 12, section 29). A complete reading of Augustine's *Confessions* could benefit a student on several fronts. As literature, it constitutes the prototype of the confessional form. A briefer Dante-focused project could comprise a little background reading about Augustine and his *Confessions*, culminating in a concentrated study of book 8. That should set up a contrast between Francesca's and Augustine's

pivotal decisions, reflecting on which, believe me, can bear a lot of fruit. My own preference was to make as strong a case as possible in class that this is an allusion to Augustine, filling in the Augustine information necessary to draw out its implications. This proved so stimulating that I put a lot of emphasis on it. It often produced some of the year's richest conversation/debate/analysis.

3. Your poetically inclined students might profit from the study of the more immediate poetic backgrounds to the *Commedia*. Poets who wrote in the Provencal or troubadour tradition abound in the first two canticles of the *Commedia*, with a few in *Inferno* and more in *Purgatorio*. These poets reflect to various degrees a stage in Dante's own development as a poet. In both substance and style, Francesca's love poem (5:100–107) brings to mind the troubadour poets and the work of a younger Dante. Her poem reminds some scholars so much of Dante's early work that they see these eight lines as an autocitation. In Dante's earlier *Vita Nuova* (Musa 2008), they find poems very close to this one. This raises a question about function. However close an approximation this poem is to Dante's earlier work, what is the point of putting in Francesca's mouth language evoking a distinct poetic style and set of doctrines about the poetry of love? This study would certainly not be every student's meat, but a few could feast on it. You might assign them general research on the Provencal poets and a specific reading of Dante's slim volume, the *Vita Nuova*. In the latter work, they will discover that Dante renounces this style of love poetry and vows not to write more on the subject until he better understands his topic. The *Commedia* constitutes the fulfillment of that vow. Such research might fashion a powerful tool for understanding how to respond to Francesca. She speaks in a poetic idiom that the maturing Dante has decided to reject. They will also learn a bit about the shadowy Beatrice in that work.

4. A greater number of your students might find Arthurian research appealing. Though a number of different versions of the Arthurian legends exist, the evidence in Francesca's reference in canto 5 points to one specific version, still extant (Corley 2008). Studying that version or just reading up on the essential story might provide students with a lot to say about the relations between the Arthur story and the Francesca/Paolo one and how an understanding of the former can sharpen our interpretive approach to the latter.

4

Structure, Person, and Emblem

CANTOS 6–9 AND 11

After a few years of teaching *Inferno* in high school, I realized that I should pair it with Camus's *The Stranger* or *The Plague*. You couldn't want a sharper counterpoint between two opposing world views. I could set Dante's intricately ordered, spiritually binding divine creation against Camus's indifferent universe. For Dante, God structures meaning into his created world; to Camus, meaning is never built in but always made by human choosing. A student of mine caught the difference succinctly in a wide-eyed comment one day in class: "Camus's universe has no circles."

Dante's cosmos teems with circles, terraces, spheres, and other images of order. The circles of *Inferno* reflect God's ranked classification of sins from least to most serious. The *Inferno*'s most comprehensive discussion of the logic behind this arrangement occurs in canto 11, where Virgil pauses to lecture Dante on hell's general design. According to Virgil, the sins in *Inferno* are measured by degree of offense to God (11:84). He explains that hell as a whole has a tripartite structure with three broad categories of sin, probably corresponding to the three beasts in canto 1. The circles between the gates of hell in canto 3 and the walls of dis in 9 comprise upper hell. There God punishes sins of incontinence, those committed by people who could not control their appetites in the world above. These sins are separated from those of lower hell spatially by the walls of dis and spiritually by the absence of malice. The sins of the incontinent are less offensive to God because they lack malice. Unlike the sinners inside the walls of dis, those in upper hell had no intention of hurting others. The damage they did in life was a byproduct of their lack of self-control. The malicious sinners in lower hell are further subdivided into two categories: the violent, who harmed others aggressively, and the fraudulent, who did so deceptively.

To penetrate very deeply God's structural logic as Dante depicts it in the poem, you'll need to discover his standards of measure. Wherever items are logically arranged in *Inferno*, that is, nearly everywhere, your students can profit by discerning what yardstick God must have used as the basis for that arrangement. By what gauge is one sin better or worse than another in any of *Inferno*'s schemes of order? Some form of logic has to apply: in *Inferno* anyway, Dante's God is relentlessly rational. At least that's a good working assumption. He has reasons for the forms of order he creates, reasons that are at least potentially intelligible to human understanding. But in the poem, as in our real world outside it, divine reasoning is at best implicit. It has to be inferred. That puts serious readers of *Inferno* in exactly the same position as theists anytime: trying to infer benign meaningfulness behind the worlds of nature and human experience. Your students will be engaging in a form of inquiry with a long and venerable history. And by understanding God's thinking in the poem, they'll be understanding Dante's.

What, then, is the standard by which adultery in *Inferno* 5 is less offensive to God than, say, counterfeiting in *Inferno* 29–30? The latter, a form of fraud, is in the most offensive category, we learn from Virgil in canto 11, because it perverts our power to reason, that faculty which separates humans from other species. One gauge might derive from the classical three-part soul idea. Plato and other classical thinkers divided the soul into appetites, willful emotions, and reason. Dante may be using some version of this analysis to stratify the three levels of hell. He consigns the incontinent to upper hell as defilers of their appetites alone, the violent to lower hell for defiling their appetites and will, the fraudulent to lowest hell as defilers of all three parts of their souls. If so, the standard is degree of corruption: the more of his soul that a sinner corrupts by his choices in life, the lower the placement in hell. So the soul of a Francesca, dominated by the appetite for sex, is less completely corrupted than that of a counterfeiter, who uses his intellect deceptively and maliciously to satisfy his desires. Hence she is logically less blameworthy, though she still has to spend eternity in agony.

Tone up your students' inferential muscle by using the yardstick question on cantos 3 through 9, in which incontinent souls in upper hell are ranked from least to most damnable. What is God's basis for this ranking? To give them a better shot at responding to this challenging question, you may want to allow them a small sin of omission. If you let them exclude the logically vexatious vestibule and limbo cantos (3 and 4) as not belonging to upper hell proper, the remaining circles down to the walls of Dis might more easily fall in place under some general rule. By what standard of measurement is the movement from lust in 5 to gluttony in 6 to avarice in 7 to wrath/sullenness in 7 and 8 a progression toward greater seriousness of sin?

I think your students will find this a difficult but stimulating question. (Such questions implicitly credit their intelligence. This can activate a kind of self-fulfilling cycle: your implied compliment leads them to respond energetically and thus to justify its terms.) In class discussion, expect them to try out a variety of answers. Though no certainty is possible in exercises like this, there certainly are tests a good answer has to pass: compatibility with the text in these cantos, with what Dante shows of his thinking elsewhere, and with the essentials of Christian thinking in general. Even though your results are bound to be inconclusive, maybe because they are, you will be fostering wholesome cultivation of the classroom garden.

The best response I've seen to this incontinence question takes seriously the idea that God is love. It assumes that being made in the image of God makes the power to love fundamental to a good human life, and thinks of sins throughout *Inferno* as corruptions or perversions of our God-given power to love. The greater the corruption of that fundamental power, the greater the sinful result. This logic might make sense of why to Dante's God Ciacco the glutton is below Francesca the adulteress, with the unrecognizable money hoarders lower yet. Pushing this, or any, approach in class can spawn objections from your students, sometimes pretty spirited ones. Hope that it does. However you come by it, studious wrangling over a challenging text like this has to be good for your classroom.

A second prominent feature of this section of the poem is more literary than theological. It too could be considered structural, since it involves a broad contrast of methods of characterization. I'm pointing to Dante's use of what Hollander calls monsters. Cantos 6 through 9 abound in mythological figures— Cerberus, Plautus, Phlegyas, the Furies, and Medusa—who challenge the pilgrim's passage through hell. Functionally, these figures need to be distinguished from the human characters Dante meets along the way, though a few of the latter are also based in mythology. Boundaries almost never run perfectly straight in this poem, but drawing this distinction as sharply as possible can tell you a lot about Dante the artist, the student of classical antiquity and ultimately the philosophical thinker.

By placing Cerberus in canto 6 next to Francesca on one side and Ciacco on the other, Dante invites comparison between two types of literary being. You will sense right away that in mode of presentation, beast and human fall into different categories. Compared to either human, Cerberus lacks substance. Though seemingly ferocious, he acts as little more than a pasteboard, or maybe neon, announcement of the content of his domain. He reminds me a little of the silhouette of a steaming coffee cup on the sign over my favorite coffee shop. No mistaking what is served there. Similarly, the three-headed dog is basically a two-dimensional advertisement that canto 6 showcases unrestrained appetite, which in our age might be interpreted to include not just gluttony but all forms of out-of-control consumption. Cerberus' only action, to flay the sinners in his circle, merely gives external form to the mutilating effects of appetite in the souls of voracious consumers.

Though they now lack physical existence, Francesca and Ciacco add mass to the representation of a sin. Francesca, as the human embodiment of the sin of lust, presents it with much of the complexity, ambiguity, physicality, and self-deception with which it occurs in real life. Signposts may be useful tools for identification and navigation, but Dante doesn't confuse them with the way moral ideas direct real human lives. No ideas but in things, one is tempted to conclude. That might place Dante with the Christian Aristotelians, which seems apt given his tribute to Aristotle in limbo "the master of those who know" (4:131) and his enthusiasm for the philosophy of Thomas Aquinas. These three great thinkers shared a suspicion of disembodied ideas. Something very important is at stake here. In an age when the sheer amount of information to be digested can be overwhelming, we all have to work at remembering that not even the loftiest ideas occur outside of a context. In public discourse these days, unanchored abstractions like freedom are tossed around like Frisbees. Good citizenship depends on learning not to factor out the context in which such terms are embedded. So does the development of high-school minds. Disregard of context spawns sentimentality, which can leave its subjects vulnerable to manipulation. Recorded history testifies repeatedly to the dangers of that. Dante's human carriers of ideas like lust or gluttony can help spur your students toward more mature thinking about the ideas that shape their lives.

You might want names for the two categories. To that end, think of representation techniques in literature as spread over a continuum, with the mythological creatures in *Inferno* at one end and the human transgressors at the other. For the latter category, you'd need a term that is nearly the opposite of "personified abstraction," the phrase scholars use to describe flat characterization typical of allegory. "Literary symbol" might be apt, but it is too cumbersome and "symbol" has been trivialized through indiscriminate use. I've struggled to find the right word, probably because, as Wayne Booth (2006) pointed out once in an absorbing essay (see the first selection), the hardest thing in the world to encompass in an adequate figure of speech is a human being. So I'll just go with "person," meaning someone in a narrative who shapes and is shaped by his environment, someone who is therefore neither simply the plaything of enormous forces, as Vonnegut (1990) puts it in *Slaughterhouse-Five* (164), nor the utter captain of his fate. Then take "person" in *Inferno* to refer to the verbal presentation of this kind of concrete man or woman, who both represents and is an instance of some idea. So Francesca is Dante's attempt to evoke the spirit of an actual historical woman with as much concrete humanness as possible in half a canto. At the same time, she acts as the representation of sinful lust. I want to define a number of the sinful characters Dante meets along his way, along with Virgil, as persons in this sense. Dante the pilgrim himself belongs in this category. My next three chapters will deal with striking examples of this mode of representation.

For the monsters, "sign?" "Icon?" "Logo?" In keeping with the coffee shop image described above, "emblem" might suffice. A monster like Cerberus is more like a line drawing of a kind sinful human excess than a fully drawn character whom no concept or type can subsume. This is to say that, among the monsters, allegorical function predominates. They don't all seem monstrous either, until you consider that the human penchants they represent, given dominion over a human soul, might well produce grossly deformed beings. But among them, of course, Dante introduces some variation. While Cerberus the voracious, Plautus the wealth-driven, and Phlegyas the irate are pretty blatant emblems of what they represent, the Furies and Medusa are harder to pin down.

The commentaries I've read reach nothing like a consensus about the Furies in *Inferno* 9. In classical literature, they are three hideous sisters who pursue and punish violators of ancient laws related to blood guilt. In *Inferno*, they threaten Dante and Virgil from the walls of Dis, blocking the pilgrim's passage into lower hell until an angel arrives to drive them away and open the gate. These may be the salient facts, but I doubt you will be satisfied to rest in them. Such lurid but thinly developed figures push you naturally toward allegory. Some commentators believe that the three sisters stand for three kinds of evil—in thought, word, and deed. Identifications like this aren't very satisfying. Consistency with *Inferno*'s previous mythological monsters and with the allegorical structure of the poem obliges you to see the Furies as representing destructive potentials in the human soul, analogous to gluttony and avarice. A good answer to the Furies question would have to point to an inner condition that feels threatening, has the power to block spiritual development, and is consistent with the mythological roles the Furies play in classical literature.

In her edition of *Inferno*, Dorothy Sayers' (1950) interpretation of the Furies satisfies all these conditions. She characterizes them literally as "avenging goddesses who haunted those who had committed great crimes." Allegorically, she sees them as "the image of the fruitless remorse which does not lead to penitence" (127). Though she offers no explanation for this inference, you don't have to be a theologian to come up with your own. She seems to think that you can become so buried in feelings of moral guilt as to put yourself beyond the reach of God's forgiveness. Then guilt can't lead to the repentance that is critical to the ability to move forward on the Christian path. This approach seems consistent with the Furies' role in both classical mythology and canto 9.

I'd like to try out an interpretation of the Furies similar to Sayers's but with a few modifications of my own. In classical literature, the Furies' most vivid appearance occurs in the *Oresteia* by the Greek playwright Aeschylus (Fagles 1984). In the last two plays of that trilogy, the Furies act as agents of a kind of primitive justice. Its Latin name is *lex talionis*, meaning law of revenge. It obligates family members, in particular, to avenge the shed blood of a kinsman. The Furies' job is to make sure that this obligation is fulfilled. Orestes finds his fate bound up with the lex talionis at two different stages in the Orestes plays. His is not the happiest of lots. After threatening Orestes with death or a visit from the Furies (it's not clear which is worse), Apollo's oracle commands him to take revenge on his mother and her lover for killing his father. After he complies, a band of Furies appears to hound him toward retribution for having himself killed a family member. Blood has to be paid for with blood. The Furies will ensure proper payment, with no exceptions allowed. The resolution of Orestes's dilemma occurs in the trilogy's final play. Athena establishes a new court in Athens to administer a more sophisticated conception of justice in which mitigating circumstances can be taken into account.

This portrayal of the Furies is similar to that in Virgil's *Aeneid*, the classical source Dante knew best. Virgil generally characterizes them there as agents of inexorable fate. Given this generally consistent background, I've come to understand the Furies in Dante as emblems of a legalistic conception of moral justice, by which all sins *must* be paid for in due measure. There would be no coming back from, say, an act of adultery, no possibility of forgiveness or redemption. The assumption that there is no way out of punishment for the sinful might well arrest someone's journey toward redemption. Such pessimism would constitute a grave misreading of God's offer of forgiveness to truly repentant humans. The Furies would then represent the immobilizing belief that some negative conditions are beyond God's power to heal. This satisfies my criteria for a tenable interpretation, but so could other approaches. Some of your students might profit from researching the Furies in classical sources as a basis for coming up with their own interpretation of *Inferno* 9.

As for what Medusa represents allegorically, I find it hard to say. To be consistent with her role in mythology, you'll need an inner condition that doesn't just make progress difficult but freezes the soul in place for good. To Sayers, Medusa is "the image of the despair which so hardens the heart that it becomes powerless to repent" (127). That relates her to the Furies plausibly and satisfies most of the other criteria for a tenable interpretation of her. But I'm not sure what despair has to do with her characterization in mythology. Still it's as interesting a suggestion as I've seen in any commentary. I think you'll find anything Sayers says about Dante worth pondering.

Somewhere between emblem and person stands one of Dante's most exquisite mythological adaptations. Though her only appearance is an indirect one in canto 7, she plays such a weighty role in the *Commedia* that her name is invoked again and again in later cantos. I'm referring to Fortuna, described at length by Virgil (7:70–96) in a reprimand to the pilgrim for his ill-considered comments about her. She is hardly a monster.

Fortuna (*Tuche* in Greek) comes with a lengthy classical pedigree. Both Greek and Roman antiquity deified her. Her image in Rome included a wheel that she constantly turned. (Your students, alas, will be familiar with *Wheel of Fortune.*) I'd be surprised if comparative study didn't turn up figures analogous to her throughout the world's mythologies, so deep is the psychological need she serves. If you can name and identify the disturbing element of chance in human affairs, perhaps you can gain some control over it. We know the Romans set up cults and performed sacrifices in worship of the goddess Fortuna. The idea was that perhaps she could be won over to the worshipper's side. At times, Roman literature testifies to this hope—in his writings, Julius Caesar sometimes attributes his military successes to having gained Fortuna's favor.

In *Inferno*, Virgil's fairly lengthy description of Fortuna is in response to Dante's thoughtless tendency to align her with the other monsters. According to the pilgrim, she holds the world's goods in her *branche,* which Hollander translates as clutches, but might more literally be rendered claws. To the pilgrim, and most of unreflective mankind, she's a beast, like Cerberus, who rakes the gluttons with his claws in the putrid mud of circle 3. After passionately rebuking Dante's "foolish" and "ignorant" impression, Virgil explains that Fortuna serves God as one of his ministers. God has given her a measure of control over the sublunary sphere, the area within the circle of the moon, that is, on earth. In God's master scheme, she manages her sphere as the various angels do the heavenly spheres. She presides over worldly affairs through the turning of her wheel, on which are strapped all earth's goods and standings. In her hands, up turns to down, and vice-versa, with swift unpredictability. Her steering ensures the insecurity of wealth, position and power in the world. She is no respecter of race, blood, political status or any other form of earthly empowerment. Her actions are beyond the capacity of human wit to understand, much less to control. As a result, "she is reviled by the very ones who most should praise her."

Virgil makes clear how serious a mistake he considers this to be. This raises another challenging question for your students. It should seem logical to them that Fortuna's activities are benign, since she works for a loving God, but how this is so requires some pondering. How can a force that renders undependable the wealth you have worked so hard to accumulate or the reputation you have so painstakingly shepherded be considered benevolent? Though, as usual, various answers are possible, the key probably lies in resolving the paradox that some fundamental insecurities can be good for you.

One further dimension of Fortuna's characterization completes her picture in an appealing way. Not only does she help explain a difficult theological matter —why misfortunes can befall anybody at any time — but she models the proper way to deal with a world full of ups and downs. Her response to human curses is simply to smile and turn her wheel, not much affected by things she can't control. By complicating her this way, Dante moves her some distance from other mythological emblems throughout *Inferno*. It is a memorable exercise in literary adaptation.

Collectively, *Inferno*'s pagan appropriations reinforce a point I made previously. To Dante, the pre-Christian Greeks and Romans knew a few things. God would not have enveloped those classical predecessor cultures in complete darkness. They had intimations of many truths about the nature and activity of the divine. But since theirs was a half-light, Dante can't appropriate their mythological ideas directly. He has to modify them for use in a Christian scheme. Still, Dante's use of figures like Fortuna suggests a kind of respect for classical cultures and reverence for a God who would not have cut himself off from humans in any period of history.

Exercises

CLOSE READING

1. Dante includes one of the most intricate allusions in the poem in the scene at *Inferno* 8 (31–63). This is a good opportunity to have your students explore the relations between *Inferno* and the Bible, Dante's primary source of allusions. This one takes some setting up. Crossing the River Styx with Virgil and the boatman Phlegyas, Dante severely denounces a wrathful sinner, Filippo Argenti, who is attempting to climb into the boat. For the first time in the poem, the pilgrim increases the suffering of one of the damned souls he meets. After shoving Argenti back into the muck, Virgil praises Dante, saying "Indignant soul, blessed is she that bore you in her womb" (8:44–45).

   Many commentators see this as a reference to Luke 11:27: "Blessed is the womb that bore you" (English Standard Version 2008) This line is delivered by a woman in a crowd, praising Jesus for his teaching about expelling evil. Have them study carefully the section of Luke in which the quote occurs. They will find Jesus discoursing there on how to drive evil out of the human soul. He identifies two stages of getting one's soul in healthy order: the getting-rid-of-evil stage and the replacing-it-with-something-better stage. Without the latter, he implies, the former is worse than useless. An empty house invites unsavory tenants. Hearing this lesson in the crowd, the woman blesses the very womb that gave birth to such a teacher. It is important to note, though, that Jesus immediately corrects her saying "Blessed rather are those who hear the word of God and keep it" (Luke 11:28).

In addition to the similar phrasing, Dante's passage resembles Luke's in the image of expelling evil. Pushing back Filippo Argenti can be seen as a carrying out of Jesus's teaching, especially as Argenti allegorically represents another harmful potential in the human soul. But the line Virgil uses to praise Dante is the one Jesus corrects. As Jesus's "rather" implies that the woman's comment is misdirected, so Dante may imply some deficiency in the sentiment Virgil expresses. If so, this allusion acts as a vehicle for suggesting limitations in even the best of pagan guides.

So, how does the biblical line in its context shed light on what Dante the poet wants to communicate here? As often, you might get at this question best through character relationships. What is the implied relation here between poet and guide? Does the allusion insinuate some criticism of the guide? If so, what shortcoming in Virgil is the poet identifying here? How is any shortcoming related to Virgil's pre-Christian status? What about poet versus pilgrim? Does the poet want us to second Virgil's praise of the pilgrim's treatment of Argenti? This canto extends a little the should-the-damned-be-pitied question: does the poet believe that a Christian should treat a damned soul harshly, given that that soul is already sentenced to suffer for eternity? Your students may find this last a particularly provocative question.

Other kinds of implications from this allusion might certainly suggest themselves. Whatever you discover from comparing the biblical passage with Dante's, I'm betting you'll agree that this is allusion crafting at its finest.

2.   The *Commedia* contains many instances of direct address by the poet to his readers. In a note on canto 8 (94–96) the Hollanders generalize helpfully about the collective function of the *Commedia*'s addresses to the reader: "to forge a relationship between us and the author that makes us partners in his enterprise." *Inferno* 9: 61–63 contains one of the most prominent of these addresses:

> O you who have sound intellects,
> consider the teaching that is hidden
> behind the veil of these strange verses.

In this case, the poet expects more of us than mere partnership. Note the implied challenge: "Don't you, dear reader, number yourself among those of sound intellect? Prove it by deciphering the allegorical meaning these verses carry." Unfortunately, the critical commentary on this passage reveals nothing like a consensus on what that teaching is. There is even disagreement on reference: does the "these" point forward or backward? (See the Hollanders' useful discussion of this problem in their note to these lines.) That is, are readers to look back for hidden teaching in Virgil's putting his hands over Dante's eyes to protect him against Medusa or forward in the sounds and images accompanying the angel's approach? Like the Hollanders, I agree with the majority who favor the backward turn. The action by Virgil seems more conspicuous, dramatic, surprising, and therefore, weighty. I find myself more inclined to look for hidden teaching in Virgil's placement of his hands than in a destructive wind. And I think reading backward challenges your students to come up with an interpretation that encompasses consistently the allegorical dimensions of Medusa, the guide, and the pilgrim. So what teaching does Dante hide behind the veil of the images here?

3. So far I have said nothing about rhyme and meter in the *Inferno*, probably because prosody questions intimidate me. But let me try to point to a few simple ways to raise questions about poetic meter and poetic form. *Poetic Meter and Poetic Form*, by the way, is the title of an accessible little classic on prosody by Paul Fussell (1979). I recommend it highly. Dante composes the entire *Commedia* in a form called *terza rima* or "third rhyme", which employs three-line stanzas called tercets. Since no earlier example of this form exists, critics believe Dante invented it to use in constructing his masterwork. A regular terza rima line is hendecasyllabic. That is, it has eleven syllables, the last one being necessary to accommodate the frequency of Italian words ending in short syllables. The resulting line is basically iambic pentameter with an extra unaccented syllable at the end. Since you can't find enough of these short endings in English, most English verse translations of the *Commedia* eliminate that last short syllable, leaving readers with the familiar iambic pentameter line, more or less.

Poets writing in any regular meter can achieve special sound effects by varying the rhythmic expectations they have set up in a reader's mind. Through such variations, poets can use sound to support sense. So you ask your students, once they have gotten a feel for the basic rhythm of the *Inferno*'s iambic line, to note those places where rhythmic variation in a phrase enhances its content. Fussell's book distinguishes various ways in which metrical variation might support content, of which three are most prominent. Successive short syllables tend to quicken the pace, as in limerick meter which has a galloping (anapestic) effect. Consecutive long syllables slow a line down, adding gravity to the words in which they occur. Inversions at the beginning of a line (long-short instead of the iambic short-long) suggest a sudden or surprising shift in meaning or tone. (Fussell, chapter 3)

Suppose for example you were teaching Ciardi's *Inferno*, which employs an iambic pentameter line. (I take my next two examples from Ciardi rather than the Hollanders because Ciardi seems more intent on achieving metrical effects and because he uses rhyme.) Consider a tercet from canto 9 of his edition, the one immediately following the veiled teachings passage cited above. It marks the coming of God's angel:

> Suddenly there broke on the dirty swell
> Of the dark marsh a squall of terrible sound
> That sent a tremor through both shores of Hell. (9:61–63)

In what particular places in these lines could you make a case that variation of meter reinforces sense or emotional tenor? You students might point to "Suddenly," which begins on an accented syllable, a down beat that is appropriate to the change of subject matter initiated here. An angel's approach is making itself felt. By giving extra weight to that first syllable, a good reader would capture some of the transitional power behind this "suddenly." Elsewhere, there are two phrases that receive extra metrical weight because Ciardi lines up two consecutive long syllables. You read "dark marsh" and "both shores" a bit more slowly than usual, giving them a little more gravity in sound. I'm betting your students can easily mount a convincing argument in both cases that the extra emphasis is justified. (I hope you will be satisfied with that. Shouldn't literary interpretation be less about positing Truth than making convincing cases? Less like appearing on quiz bowl than, say, wrangling with Socrates in the marketplace.)

In rhyme scheme, *Inferno*'s terza rima form features an interlocking structure. The first and third lines of a tercet rhyme, with the middle line rhyming with the first and third lines of the following tercet. The rhyme scheme is then aba, bcb, cdc, and so on. The form thus creates a kind of energetic push, since each tercet contains an unrhymed line awaiting completion in the next tercet. Thus Dante uses sound to drive readers forward through his poem. This scheme creates problems for English translators. A rhyme-poor language like English just can't provide the unlimited supply of triple rhymes that the form requires. Most translators have been willing to settle for less. Like the Hollanders and Allen Mandelbaum (1981), they leave aside rhyme altogether and opt for something like blank verse. Or like Ciardi, they catch the double rhyme in each tercet and forget trying to rhyme that troublesome middle line. Among those editions I've studied, only Dorothy Sayers's attempts to deliver the complete terza rima form. It is instructive to study the result. I doubt you will be satisfied with it, so often does the triple rhyme force her into awkward and convoluted expressions. You lose a lot by dropping Dante's interlocking rhyme in English, but a lot more by trying to maintain it. Robert Pinsky (1993) takes a middle path by keeping the rhyme scheme but expanding the boundaries of what will count as rhyme. He includes any parallel consonant or vowel sound at the end of two words. With that modification, his translation approximates full terza rima.

Because rhyme links two words by sound, poets can use that linkage, at least occasionally, to connect content or implication in the rhymed words. It therefore makes sense to ask where and how poetic meaning is enriched by connecting the ideas in a pair of rhymed words. Obviously not all rhymes will respond to this kind of questioning. But from any rhymed translation you can supply your students with many pairs or trios that might. This will teach them to see rhyme as not just ornamental but, at least at times, expressive. Here's another tercet from canto 9 with a candidate for meaningful rhyme. Virgil is warning the pilgrim against looking at Medusa:

> Volgiti 'n dietro e tien lo viso chiuso
> Che se 'l Gorgon si mostra e tu 'l vedessi,
> Nulla sarebbe di tornar mai suso.

Unless the pilgrim keeps his eyes *chiuso*, "closed" now, he will lose any chance of ever moving *suso*, "up" toward the light again. Ciardi's translation mimics this rhymed effect:

> Turn your back and keep your eyes shut tight;
> for should the Gorgon come and you look at her,
> never again would you return to the light. (55–57)

You could claim that rhyming *chiuso* with *suso* or "tight" with "light" helps to highlight a paradox: on a journey like this one, darkness and light may not always be contradictory images. In this case the darkness behind shut eyes is critical to Dante's forward and eventually upward movement. Though Dante's education in *Inferno* depends on a lot of close scrutiny of the inhabitants of hell and their contrapassos, some things are better not seen. Dante the poet may be pointing out the naïveté of the humanist conception of an education in which all subjects are open to enquiry with no holds barred. Resolving this paradox might be a key to understanding Medusa's role in the poem. If so, then Dante's and Ciardi's rhyme connecting contraries in sound serves a meaningful function.

I feel you leaning forward to point out that one can't really draw such conclusions about translations. Meter and rhyme can't be translated between any two languages in anything like point-by-point correspondence. So when you raise questions about meter and rhyme regarding Ciardi's translation, you will get answers that apply as much or more to Ciardi than to Dante. This is undeniable. To this charge I say "so be it." The alternative is to avoid altogether questions about poetic form when studying translations of the old great non-English narrative poems. That's too great a price to pay. So I hope you will grant poetic status to verse *Infernos* like Ciardi's, the Hollanders', and Pinsky's. Most modern translators of the *Commedia* have been pretty accomplished poets in their own right. Their translations of *Inferno* are poems; they deserve to be read poetically.

4.   In almost any canto of *Inferno*, you can raise the contrapasso question: how does divine cause and effect work in the case of the gluttons, the greedy, or the emotionally incontinent? In any of these cases, will the text support an argument that the suffering is not so much a punishment imposed by God as a revelation of what a human has made of his soul by the time he dies?

THEMES AND ISSUES

1.   You might develop the contrast between Ciacco and Cerberus as images of gluttony. Use this contrast to get at the difference between two modes of representation, what I'm calling personal versus emblematic presentation. Ask your students what distinguishes these two figures representing the same transgression, why any differences matter, and why the poet so often employs both methods of presenting an idea. Make them ground any arguments they offer in specific references to the text. As I've suggested, here's an area where literary technique has implications of great importance to your students. They can begin to realize how convenient it is to flatten out the world in thought to make it manageable, or to blithely accept the manipulative flattenings of others, and how the best literature acts as a corrective to that tendency.

2.   Or you could spend some time interpreting specific mythological figures. The Furies and Medusa will have grotesque appeal, but Fortuna might

offer the greatest rewards to your students. How can such a ruthless wheel turner be the agent of a loving God? How is Dante's placement of her description—between the greedy and the irate sinners—meaningful? How does her behavior under human blaming and defaming support the idea behind her divine appropriation? More generally (and this might entail a little research), how do other religions/philosophies/cultures deal with the unpredictable vicissitudes of human life? Relative to other conceptions, how compelling is Dante's Christian Fortuna figure?

3.   The structure question: By what measure does Dante's God rank as increasingly blameworthy the incontinent sinners in circles 2 through 5? More generally, what are the implications of a divinely created hell with such elaborate logical structure? What distinguishes Dante's understanding of God and his creation from that of other Christian writers? From other theistic conceptions (Muslim, Jewish, Hindu)? From the vision of an absurdist like Camus?

Research

1.   Your students might enjoy researching the backgrounds of any of the classical mythological figures Dante uses in *Inferno*. For cantos 6 through 9, the most interesting choices are probably the Furies, Medusa, and Fortuna. I know of two handy places to begin this research. *The Oxford Classical Dictionary* (Hornblower, Spawforth, and Eidinow 2012) offers authoritative summary articles on many mythological figures. Robert Graves' (1993) two-volume *The Greek Myths* provides a more comprehensive survey of the characterizations of all the important Greek mythological figures, accompanied by a thorough listing of original sources. Among other rewards, reading Graves will show your students how much variation there was in a body of narratives founded in oral tradition. Your students could write up their findings according to various formats or present them in class as a means of addressing two kinds of questions: how given mythological figures function in specific cantos and what they reveal about Dante's Christian take on classical antiquity.

Extension

This might be a good place in your course to create a lesson focused on sentimentalization in the representation of objects, in both literature and life. I'm referring to the potentially dangerous kind where someone manipulatively creates a one-sided, emotion-steeped image of something in order to gain an advantage, not to the affectionate, relatively innocuous, rosy aura in which people often cloak favorite relatives, friends, lovers, or pets.

Though contemporary instances of the former abound in public life, particularly in the political domain, let me cite my favorite literary expression of what I mean. It occurs with the Grangerford family in *Huckleberry Finn*. The Southern aristocratic ideal by which the Grangerfords appear to live certainly has its appeal—in the highly ordered, mannerly, and respectful family life it engenders, in the hospitality it requires to strangers like Huck, and especially in the soft-spoken, kindly authority of Colonel Grangerford himself. At first, Huck finds the family pretty impressive. But it doesn't take Twain long to reveal the less savory underpinnings of the their way of life: a hierarchy privileging Southern gentlemen like Colonel Grangerford at the top supported by slave labor at the bottom, with women somewhere in the decorative middle, as lovely adornments to the household and not much more. The whole edifice is held in place emotionally by a code of honor that has fueled an endless feud with a rival family. The cost of this code reveals itself to Huck when he finds his young friend Buck Grangerford lying dead in the water at the edge of the Mississippi, an adolescent casualty of the chivalric ethic of his class. Here Twain exploits the ironic distance between appearance and reality to provide readers with all the elements of pernicious sentimentalization: a two-dimensional picture held in place by emotional appeals that tend to suppress critical evaluation in order to privilege some individuals or groups over others personally, socially, economically, or politically.

The Grangerford episode thus illustrates one of the greatest benefits good literature can offer your students. It can sharpen their ability to recognize irony and ambiguity. It thus helps cultivate in them the remedy for exploitative forms of sentimentality: the habit of trying to see public phenomena, at least, as much in the round as possible. Good books like *Huckleberry Finn* encourage the kind of objective analysis and consideration of consequences that are essential to mature participation in a democratic society.

Of course, any capable writer can provide you with fodder for discussion of literary verisimilitude, but Dante's counterbalancing of thoroughly human representations ("persons") with allegorical abstractions ("emblems") offers you a particularly valuable opportunity. Armed with increased awareness, your students will find their public culture awash in sentimentalized objects. Having them reclaim some of these objects for classroom perusal can be stimulating and fun. I don't know enough about history to judge how high our culture ranks on the sentimentality scale, but modern information technology certainly makes opportunities to flatten, distort and sentimentalize objects more abundant than ever. If students do not develop the power of standing back reflectively from sentimentalized forms of manipulation, modernity's overwhelming tide of words and images threatens to carry their minds away.

5

Three Literary Persons

CANTOS 10, 13, AND 15

Canto 10: Faction

In his canto 11 survey of hell's structure, Virgil analyzes lower hell as follows:

> 'Every evil deed despised in Heaven
> has as its end injustice. Each such end
> harms someone else through either force or fraud.
>
> But since the vice of fraud is man's alone,
> it more displeases God, and thus the fraudulent
> are lower down, assailed by greater pain. (11:22–27)

What separates lower from upper hell then is malice: the intention to do unjust harm to others, which is carried out in destructive deeds. The poem subdivides lower hell into the circles of violence and of fraud, the latter being worse because peculiarly human. Pilgrim and guide visit the circles of fraud beginning in canto 17. By canto 10, they have passed through the gates of dis and into the sixth circle at the threshold of the circles of the violent in circle 7 (analogous in positioning to the pagans in canto 4 in relation to the following circles of the incontinent).

Dante builds canto 10 around a striking example of what I'm calling a literary "person." Farinata degli Uberti, the famous thirteenth-century Ghibelline chieftain, dominates the canto. To understand the politics animating his characterization, you'll need to read up a little on Guelphs and Ghibellines, the two Florentine political parties whose violent opposition led to a series of battles for dominance in thirteenth-century Italy. Any good edition of *Inferno* will supply you with enough contemporary political background to get you through the poem. That information will be useful at many points, but nowhere more than in this canto. You'll sense that for the poem's earliest Florentine readers, a confrontation between an eminent Guelph like Dante and a great Ghibelline leader might have had considerable punch. The prominence of political issues in a religious poem should come as no surprise. Its author spent the last twenty years of his life in forced exile from Florence due to political upheaval there.

Structurally, Dante's encounter with Farinata initiates a new section of the poem. As the first sinner Dante meets inside the walls of Dis, Farinata is located close to but separate from the violent, who exercised aggressive malice toward their neighbors, themselves (by suicide), or God. Though Farinata was no stranger to overt violence in his life, his damnable offense is more intellectual than physical. Dante and Virgil find him entombed with the Epicureans. From the elaborate philosophical system developed by Epicurus and his disciples, Virgil singles out disbelief in the soul's immortality as the basis for the condemnation of these heretics. This raises a placement question. How is heretical belief, particularly of the sort that Virgil identifies here, deserving of location in lower hell, in association with, if not among, the malicious?

Answering that question will certainly entail knowing something about Epicurus and his many followers. As always, you can find an authoritative summary of Greek and Roman Epicureanism in the *Oxford Classical Dictionary* (Hornblower, Spawforth, and Eidinow 2012). See also the fascinating recent discussion of Lucretius's thought in Stephen Greenblatt's (2012) *The Swerve*. Though Epicurus was a third-century BCE Greek, the best extant primary source development of his thought is surely *The Nature of Things* (Stallings, 2007) by the great Roman poet Lucretius (ca 99–55 BCE), a work that Dante knew well. Your students could develop this connection into a good research project of about any size.

Epicureans were basically materialists for whom happiness, by which they usually meant pleasure, was the highest good. Rather than uproarious self-indulgence, their hedonism commonly led to a simple life in retirement, to emphasis on dependable pleasures like friendship and on the attainment of tranquility, and to practical reflection on the causality of pleasure and pain. Epicureans often criticized established religion for beliefs that heightened the fear of death. Their practice focused primarily on the careful philosophical dismantling of the machinery of that fear. Classical history includes among the followers of this philosophy a number of illustrious Greeks and Romans.

In his characterization of Farinata in canto 10, Dante tries to do some justice to the historical weight of Epicurean personalities. Farinata is arguably hell's most imposing post-limbo figure. Here, for one of the few times in *Inferno*, Virgil directs Dante to approach a sinner respectfully. He finally has to force the pilgrim to face the shade of Farinata as he rises halfway out of his tomb. His are the "chest and brow" of a formidably proud and commanding personality, so self-possessed that he can look upon his suffering with scorn. His mere voice is enough to unnerve the cowering pilgrim. A few lines later, Farinata reminds Dante of the time after the Battle of Montaperti in 1260 when he alone prevented the destruction of Florence by victorious members of his own Ghibelline party. At line 73, as Farinata resumes speaking, the poet terms him *magnanimo*, great-souled, the term by which Aristotle identifies one of the most admirable of human qualities. In light of these details, it would be hard to deny that Dante wants to give some credit to this figure and the philosophy to which he is linked. Farinata's, again, is no single-dimensional picture. Think Achilles or maybe the wartime Charles de Gaulle: powerful, charismatic, and profoundly ambiguous.

But Farinata now resides pretty uncomfortably in hell. As with other sins, Dante presents heresy not just as an abstraction but as it is incorporated in a historical personality. The resulting Epicurus/Farinata compound is rich with implications. The poet can display the general consequences of this heresy in the contrapasso and particularize some of them to suit the characterization of Farinata. In the literal contrapasso, God has entombed "more than a thousand" Epicurean souls at death together in a red hot coffin lying above ground with the lid removed. Out of the opening issues "lamentation . . . from wretches in despair and pain." (9:122–23) Being allowed to rise up briefly, waist-high, from their tomb must only increase these souls' torment by sharpening their recognition of their own confinement.

As with any instance of the contrapasso, you could interpret these images according to the logic of retributive punishment. Because Epicureans denied the immortality of the soul, they have to spend eternity in a tomb as if they were mortal. God's poetic justice. Because Epicurean thought focuses primarily on the self's own pleasures and pains, Farinata now finds himself crammed together incommunicado with a great throng of like-minded souls, with whom his selfish philosophy would have prevented much genuine human contact. Lives of pleasure-seeking have led to an afterlife of unremitting pain. And so on. I find such reasoning, though interpretively defensible, unappealing because it casts God as some kind of wittily ironic bill collector.

The allegorical geography of the human soul I outlined in previous chapters may offer you a more satisfying approach. Then a soul's situation after death reveals the shape it gave itself in life. What I'm calling shape is a spatial metaphor. I could as well have used medical imagery. Then healthy/unhealthy would define the continuum on which a soul's choices in life place it. Whatever figure you choose, you'll have to develop its connection to the Christian idea of repentance. Dante situates repentant souls in purgatory, the second canticle of the *Commedia*. Relatively healthy, well-shaped souls *are* purgatorial: in them real repentance, already a step toward purgation, can take place. Unhealthy, misshapen souls bend toward hell. They have only a theoretical chance to repent, so immured are they in some incontinent, violent, or fraudulent disposition. Death merely projects the results of their soul-making in hellish imagery on a visual screen. Then God is not some cosmic source of clever punishment but the loving creator of a just and meaningful universe. I'm belaboring these claims because I think they offer you the best opportunity to do justice to Dante's thinking in a way that can appeal broadly to your students.

Then the Epicurean flaming coffin would convey the unveiled truth of what living by that heresy does to a soul. It doesn't offer much comfort or room for movement. Though a primary purpose of any philosophical perspective must be to liberate, Dante seems to believe that following Epicurus will ultimately have the opposite effect. Apparently a materialistic disbelief in the soul's immortality closes down rather than opening up, confines rather than liberates, and brings pain rather than solace, let alone joy and understanding. Farinata's rising up and looking around suggests the opportunity to envision a larger picture. Even before the Christian dispensation, Epicureans had access to classical traditions crediting the immortality of the soul. Hence Dante holds them responsible for not being able to keep from falling back into their old, painfully confining viewpoint. This underlies Dante's distinction between the fiery pagan coffin here and the green meadows of pagan limbo. Why a Christian thinker should single out this particular classical school of thought for such harsh criticism will not be hard for you and your students to work out. Only note that this is an exercise in reasoning, not thoughtless dismissal. What exactly is it about even the most thoughtful form of hedonistic materialism that would cause a Christian thinker to depict it through the imagery of an inflamed coffin?

For a possibly enriching allusion, have a student read aloud in class the third tercet of canto 10, in which the pilgrim poses a question to his guide:

> The souls that lie within the sepulchers,
> may they be seen? For all the lids are raised
> and there is no one standing guard.

Some of your students are bound to hear a biblical echo here. They will relate these images to the description of the tomb of Jesus on Easter morning, which the two Marys find empty, unguarded, and with the entrance-covering stone rolled away. The allusion would then be comparing the condition of Farinata's soul after death with that of the resurrected Jesus, which shows no such confinement, no such pain, no such reason for lamentation. Encourage your students to discover these and other contrasts through which Dante adds force to what he wants to communicate about a great Epicurean.

Some of Farinata's personal characteristics soon begin to mar an otherwise impressive-looking countenance. His is the language of snooty factionalism. His default attitude toward his impinging surroundings here, as it no doubt was in life, is "utter scorn." Only Dante's Tuscan "courtesy of speech" and the Ghibelline's nagging concerns about Florentine politics gain the pilgrim an audience. Farinata greets with barely concealed disdain Dante's answer to what must be his standard conversation opener: a pompous demand for proof of pedigree. You first have to prove to this guy that you are worth addressing. His question also seems to act as his device for bringing up what does interest him: "me, my forebears, and my party" (10:47). Ghibelline clan pride expresses itself repeatedly in his conversation with the pilgrim, but nowhere more incriminatingly than in his reaction to the shade of Cavalcanti, a Guelph aristocrat with whom he shares his tomb. For eternity. Farinata shows not a trace of sympathy toward a man who, in addition to the pains of punishment, is tormented by lack of knowledge about his son's condition in the world above. You'd think a father's concerns would resonate with a clan-proud figure like Farinata, but this "magnanimous" spirit never acknowledges Cavalcanti's presence. As often, Dante uses what a character doesn't do to lay open who he is.

The poet apparently wants to associate an Epicurean perspective with selfish narrowness of vision. It seems that to Dante a this-worldly hedonist lifestyle wears away humane sympathy and undermines standards of restraint. Living the Epicurean life might then be seen as an act of intellectual violence against natural fellow feeling, against the humbling recognition that human beings are vulnerable and incomplete in their understanding, and against any idea that there might exist a larger world in time or space than what earthly desires account for.

Arguably, like most other cantos, this one has a unifying theme. I'd call it synecdoche, that figure of speech in which a part is substituted for the whole. This comes out in the confused pilgrim's closing question about the damned souls' knowledge of time. Farinata explains that enough of "the Ruler's light still shines" for the heretics to enable them to see at a distance, that is to see the future, but not the present. So Farinata can accurately predict Dante's exile from Florence in a few years, but Cavalcanti can't know whether his son is still alive now, in the year 1300. Thus Epicureans (and maybe all hell dwellers—the text is not clear about this) see only part of time's unfolding. When Dante conveys to Virgil his anxiety about Farinata's grim prophecy, the guide replies in effect: "that man may see something about your future, but he can envision only a part of the picture of your life. Later you will receive a complete prophecy from a reliable source [Beatrice] who radiates the light of heaven." Farinata is everywhere guilty of the sin of partiality: substituting worldly life for the here and beyond, pleasure on earth for the fulfillment of the spirit, clan and faction for human-kind, and various kinds of partial seeing for complete knowledge. This seems to be Dante's ultimate take on the Epicurean heresy: while there is nothing wrong with pleasure in itself, it becomes vicious when not grounded in a larger picture that gives it proper subordinate meaning. In a way, all of *Inferno* is about making things ultimate that should rightly be subordinate. Making pleasure the ultimate end confines, reduces, and impoverishes a human being until he is a mere part detached from the whole. For the opposite of such detachment, I refer you again to the closing image of *Paradiso* in which a matured pilgrim feels himself in gear with the divine love that "moves the sun and the other stars."

Canto 13: Negation

Can a suicide ever be considered noble? Dante's answer to this question might surprise your students. Though canto 13 visits the wood of the suicides and focuses on an elaborate portrait of Pier delle Vigne, a well-known Italian who killed himself in 1249, Dante locates at least one famous suicide elsewhere. The position of this pre-Christian Roman in purgatory emphasizes again that, to Dante, God is not rule-bound. As soon as you think you have understood his patterns of judgment, Dante's God will make some move that shakes up your thinking. In trying to find a coherent place for God's more puzzling moves, as Dante envisions them, you and your students can learn a lot about the human predilection for categorizing. The fun in the *Commedia* often lies in grappling with the exceptions.

He thus finds a place in purgatory, the gateway to heaven, for Cato the Younger, a famous senatorial defender of the Roman Republic against the imperial ambitions of Julius Caesar. In the first two cantos of *Purgatorio*, Cato acts as a kind of guardian of the Mountain of Purgatory, shepherding upward the repentant souls whom an angel ferries to its base. Your students will want to question Dante's placement of him on two counts: he was a pagan who lived before the time of Christ (95–46 BCE) and so at best should reside in limbo; he committed suicide and would therefore seem to belong here in canto 13. Can God be so poor a logician as to contradict himself twice in one figure? Theologically, that obviously won't wash, so one has to look for some explanation in which Cato's presence in purgatory is not ultimately paradoxical.

Cato's life is worth studying. One Roman epic, Lucan's *Civil War* (Fox 2012), deals with the death throes of the Roman republic during which Cato dignifies himself and his republican cause by militarily opposing Julius Caesar. Lucan's narrative ends before Caesar's defeat of the republican armies in the Battle of

Thapsus in 46 BCE, after which Cato committed suicide rather than be captured. Consult Plutarch's *Life of Cato* (Dryden 1992) for the most vivid account of this famous act. To Cato, Caesar's victory meant the end of Roman *libertas*, an outcome he found intolerable. Students interested in Roman military and political history, stoic philosophy, or the backgrounds to Dante's thought would probably find reading either of these two works profitable. But even a little discussion of Cato in the context of *Inferno* 13 could lead to two potentially enlightening questions for your students. What differences between Cato at the base of the mountain of purgatory and Pier delle Vigne in the wood of suicides might justify their disparate placements in the *Commedia*? Ditto for Cato and Socrates, Plato, or Aristotle in *Inferno* 4? This will be an exercise in making careful distinctions. You may be able to mark it down as some of that critical thinking that educational reformers are always deploring the lack of. Here's hoping that your students won't get through *Inferno* without a lot of that.

To distinguish Pier from Cato, you'll naturally tend to look for differences in motivation for the suicidal act. You may find that unlike Cato, Pier has the mind of a suicide. As usual, Dante provides a variety of clues, external and internal to the character, to lead you to something like this conclusion. You might point out to your students the frequency of the Italian "non" as a sentence opener in the first three tercets of the canto. They usher readers into a pathless forest, well-suited to sinners whose ultimate pronouncement was "no." The description of the foliage in the second tercet

> No green leaves, but those of dusky hue—
> not a straight branch, but knotted and contorted—
> no fruit of any kind, but poisonous thorns.

reinforces the atmospheric negativity of this place by implying that things unnatural and unhealthy grow here. The presence of the Harpies intensifies this effect. Classical mythology represents them as disgusting bird-women, sometimes pictured as dripping with excrement, who snatch food and deliver dire but often misleading prophecies. In book 3 of Virgil's *Aeneid* (Day Lewis 1953, 3:225–58), the Harpies swoop in to pollute the feast of Aeneas and his hungry men. Then they prophesy that before these Trojan refugees can establish their city, they will suffer such hunger as to have to eat their very tables. In a way this prediction comes true, but only if the meaning of "tables" is stretched almost beyond recognition.

Classical literature could hardly provide Dante with better emblems of the spirit of negation than the Harpies. In canto 13, these vile creatures nest in the twisted branches of trees that house the souls of Pier and the other suicides. Like other mythological figures in *Inferno*, they can represent a tendency lodged in every human soul. It is sadly appropriate that the Harpies' lamentations provide the background audio for the canto and that through wounding they provoke the tree souls to painful, bloody communication. Dante implies that what leads to suicide in the first place is the inability to keep the language of Harpy-like negativity from drowning out the better voices of our nature. To Dante, a suicidal mind must be one whose default setting is deeply pessimistic: my feast will always be spoiled; my future will be dismal; my environment is set up to wound me. Minds given over to such poisonous certainties become unnaturally sickly, twisted, knotted up. The act of suicide, which is finally a piece of communication through one's own blood, is the culmination of this state of mind taken to an extreme. Pier's must have been such a mind. For one kind of opposite to the suicidal mentality in the poem, look to the image of Fortuna in canto 7—she who when the outside world hurls curses at her simply, confidently, and joyfully plays her divinely assigned role. For another, consider Cato.

In discussing this canto, you might ask your classes to think about the basic emotional quality coloring the speech of the people they know best. What spirit typically moves them to communicate? If your students are like mine, they will first recall those fortunate friends who convey a sense of joy in nearly everything they say. Ask students if they know anyone who regularly speaks out of a sense of his own pain. Such questioning admittedly lays bare a troubling distinction from a troubling canto. To me, that's all the more reason for discussing it.

Dante's development of Pier as an individual bears out some such analysis as the above and justifies his placement in this canto. Notice his first words: "Why do you break me? . . . Why do you tear me?" Note how Virgil addresses him: "O wounded soul." And how Pier blames the whore Envy for inflaming "all minds against me" in the court of the Holy Roman Emperor Frederick II. He claims to have killed himself to escape from the painful scorn of others at court and finally of the emperor himself. His world was out to wound him. The truth seems to be that the unbearable loss of his "glorious office" as trusted advisor to the emperor led to his suicide. You have to wonder why in this case the loss of a worldly position and subsequent imprisonment, admittedly painful and probably unjust, rendered life not worth living. Dante seems to consider this the critical question. Much hinges on Pier's relation to Frederick. Pier calls Frederick his "lord" and proudly claims that he "held both keys to Frederick's heart." Commentators have noted here the resemblance to another Peter (Pier is Peter in Italian) holding heavenly keys in service to another Lord. Dante's understanding of Pier's suicide seems to include some idea of a flawed hierarchy of allegiances. Giving absolute value to his position serving an earthly ruler was probably Pier's way of dealing with a threatening world. But this left him defenseless against Fortuna's unpredictability. The loss of his position was thus calamitous, particularly to someone with a fundamentally pessimistic mind. Dante implies that primary allegiance to a more loving, fatherly Lord might have provided Pier with the resources with which to withstand the downward turning of Fortune's wheel. Where Pier might have heard God's voice, he left himself with the wailings of Harpies.

You should pay some attention to how Pier speaks in addressing guide and pilgrim. In first identifying himself to them, he easily falls into an artificial oratorical style. Consider the inflated pride of status his introduction conveys: "*Io son colui che*," or "I am he who" (58). Ask your students when they last delivered anything like that phrase with their handshake. Even in Dante's day it must have sounded pretty stuffy. Look at the rhetorically ornate language he uses throughout his first section of speech (55–78) in which he explains the circumstances that led to his suicide Self-exculpatingly. Have your students study the Italian for the two tercets at 67–72, which could serve as a textbook on highly stylized rhetorical devices. Even if you don't go into those, your students will be able to hear, through all the tangled repetitions, the artificial, role-bound ring of Pier's language. Such embellishment might have distinguished him in Frederick's court, but it seems ridiculously out of place here. Even in hell, this man can't quit clinging to his courtly self-image.

When Pier is asked to address directly the situation of suicides in this wood (93–108), the tenor of his speech changes pretty dramatically. Abandoning pretense and self-pity, he speaks much more from his present condition. His language becomes direct, factual, and unpretentious, more appropriate to someone who now has to deal with the unornamented details of the suffering he has caused himself. I hear in these words a more appealing Pier. In confronting admittedly appalling worldly circumstances, such candor might have served him better than insistence on his status or self-pity at his mistreatment. He might have faced his situation, admitted his vulnerability, looked for solace in a better place, and ultimately avoided the negative causality that has led to a sad death and this painful position in the afterlife.

The canto closes with three additional inhabitants of the forest. The first two souls, chased and dismembered by a pack of dogs, were guilty of wasting their possessions in such a way as to commit what the Hollanders call "material suicide." More interesting is the final figure, an anonymous Florentine suicide who seems to represent the city of Florence itself. Through a century of civil strife, Florence has been making its house a gallows. Apparently cities, like individuals, can become suicidal.

The pilgrim twice expresses sympathy toward the suicides he meets. At one point Virgil has to speak to Pier for him because "I cannot, such pity fills my heart." Then in the first tercet of canto 14 he gathers and returns to the Florentine suicide his fallen leaves, "Urged by the love I bore my place of birth." Are these emotions the poet wants his reader to share? (Note that this brings up again the relation between poet and pilgrim.) Should the damned in these poignant cases be pitied? You can be pretty sure that the poet would not endorse any simplistic answers. As this canto shows, questions about how to judge another person's suicide are hard to answer. I doubt you will be able to fend them off in the classroom, though. Nor should you want to. Putting you and your students in difficult positions like this is one thing that makes great literature great.

Canto 15: Paternity

A younger man with a physical body walks with the shades of two older men. One, the guide, is positioned beside the pilgrim up on a stone dike that protects them from the fiery rain and burning sand. The other, a former mentor, briefly breaks away from a troop roaming the scorching waste to accompany the pilgrim, but below him on the sand. The pilgrim's attention focuses almost entirely on the latter to the point of rudely neglecting the former. Pilgrim and former mentor do almost all of the talking, their conversation interrupted momentarily by one pithy line from the guide, toward whom the pilgrim barely turns his head to listen. For this canto more than most others, your students will need to see what's going on. Without detailed envisioning of canto 15's choreography, they will miss a lot of its force.

Sharp visualization is important here because canto 15 paints some semblance of a family portrait, at least as much of one as you are going to find in this poem. Curiously, Dante's immediate family—parents, siblings, wife, children—get no mention in the *Commedia*. The one relative Dante does give prominence in the poem is his great-great grandfather Cacciaguida, to whom the pilgrim talks at length in *Paradiso*. Such a distant exception urges the obvious question: why, in a first-person poem covering so much personal territory, would the poet completely suppress family information closer to home? This problem has spawned a lot of commentary, all of it necessarily speculative. But one thing is sure: if you want to read the pilgrim's story in anything like a domestic frame, you are going to have to draw your materials, by inference, from other figures in the poem. In canto 15, the pilgrim is flanked by two pretty strong candidates for surrogate father: Publius Virgilius Maro and Brunetto Latini. Present guide and former mentor. An accurate visual impression of this canto's interactions thus leads to questions about paternity. Who makes the good father? Understanding the charge of sodomy against Brunetto may depend on considering this prior question. (Though the reference to the biblical Sodom might include sexually deviant behavior of any kind, let's focus here, as most commentators have, on homosexuality.)

As your *Inferno* edition will no doubt explain, Brunetto Latini (1220–94) was one of the preeminent Florentine literary, philosophical and political figures of his day. His dates show that day to have been more than a generation before Dante's. Hence many critics have doubted how literal a mentor Brunetto was to him. But there is little doubt about his influence over Dante as a thinker and a writer, even in the *Commedia*. In canto 15 you can feel the reverent affection the pilgrim has for Brunetto, especially as a literary model. By most accounts, Brunetto's two surviving major works, the *Tesoro* and the *Tesoretto*, had a major effect on Dante the aspiring young writer. Though a good deal else is known about Brunetto's life, no extant source confirms Dante's apparent indictment of Brunetto as a homosexual. Many scholars have found these facts troubling. They present readers with a disquieting dilemma: either to condemn an admired poet for contemptible treatment of a major influence in his life, or to try to find some way to deliteralize the homosexual claim to let the poet off the hook.

For *Commedia* lovers like me, it's natural to want to steer in the latter direction. My attempt to do so will not be the first. In fact I owe a lot of what I say here to a glorious National Endowment for the Humanities Summer Seminar on the Commedia I attended years ago taught by Bill Stephany, a former University of Vermont professor and Dante scholar. The liberal in me wants to argue, with some of the students in Stephany's seminar, that to the mature author of the *Commedia*, the larger picture of poor paternity is what counts here, inside which Brunetto's possible homosexuality plays at most a supporting role.

The pilgrim sums up his continuing affection for Brunetto in these words:

> For I remember well and now lament
> the cherished, kind, paternal image of you
> when, there in the world, from time to time,
> You taught me how man makes himself immortal.
> And how much gratitude I owe for that
> my tongue, while I still live, must give report. (15:81–87)

Thus he pays his respects to a man obviously to be regarded as great by worldly standards. Even Brunetto's speech in this canto expresses a gentle, sympathetic humanism that is easy to find appealing. I certainly do. Many commentators have supported the pilgrim in his evaluation of this soul here. But the still-living poet has obviously belied the pilgrim's pledge above by placing Brunetto in hell (unless you read "how much" as cutting both ways, with the pilgrim answering "a lot" but the poet replying "not as much as I thought"). To Dante the poet, worldly fame and accomplishment apparently offer no stay against damnation. Your students must look again for details that, in the context of fiery rain and burning sand, might be read ironically, places where Brunetto incriminates himself without intending to or the admiring pilgrim does it for him, details that can be read as wise by one standard and damnable by another. The key may lie in the pilgrim's word "paternal" along with the "son" by which Brunetto twice refers to Dante earlier in the canto. He seems to relish his role as father spirit to younger writers like Dante. This suggests a criterion by which he might be judged. By *Commedia* reckoning, how far does the information in this canto show Brunetto to have been a good literary father figure?

To answer this question, you'd have to draw out the implications of "paternal" in this poem. This may be a good time to prompt your students to reflect on what makes a good father anytime, biologically or figuratively. I think I can promise you that they will speak up about this in class. To Dante, the word must be tied to the nurturing of healthy growth, a conclusion I reach by reasoning negatively from what's in canto 15. He sentences Brunetto to move eternally, sometimes at a run, in a band with other men through a desert landscape inflamed above and below. Botanically, this is the image of sterility: a place where nothing natural can grow. Remembering that Dante likes to imply in a canto's setting something about the condition of the souls that dwell there, you might hypothesize that non-procreativity is thematic in this canto. Bad fathers don't foster beneficial growth in their offspring, especially when it comes to matters of ultimate importance. Good fathers, biological or literary, do.

Dante the pilgrim seems to give Brunetto paternal credit for an education not just of the pen but also of the mind and heart. Does the poet want us to agree with him? The terms of the pilgrim's praise of Brunetto provide us with some means to answer that question. He gushes forth the memory that Brunetto taught him how man "makes himself immortal" (literally *s'etterna*, or eternalizes himself). This must mean that Brunetto taught Dante how to achieve a kind of temporal immortality through his poetry. The Hollanders on this point: "he [Dante] did learn from him [Brunetto] how his earthly fame might be established by writing a narrative poem in Italian" (15:83–85n). Have your students comment on the worth of this fatherly counsel, not in the pilgrim's mind, but to the Christian poet they have learned to recognize behind these first fifteen cantos. Then you might ask the same question with the context removed. Do fathers who give top priority to worldly success foster truly healthy growth in their offspring?

It should not be surprising that Brunetto thinks he lives on in his encyclopedic work, the *Treasure* (15:119). This belief raises two questions. First, assuming Brunetto is right, what would be the nature of his particular brand of immortality? How might Dante want his readers to judge the worth of *Treasure*, a three-volume work dealing with a variety of topics including classical learning, ethics, and the principles of good government? You'd have to know a lot more about Brunetto's work than I to answer that question confidently. But I'd bet this is another case of conflicting standards of judgment, Brunetto's acknowledged worldly triumph now coming up short under the poet's loftier gaze. Dante may see the *Treasure* as taking too humanistic an approach without enough room for the play of transcendent forces. (If so, he's issuing an invitation to comparison: the *Treasure* versus the *Commedia* in substance and especially in purpose.) The second concern would point to the brand of infernal immortality that Brunetto is presently experiencing in the poem. His *Treasure* statement seems to neglect this, just as that work itself might have discounted supernatural causes. Shouldn't Brunetto's present "charred" condition in hell figure more than it does in his statement about immortality?

You may develop similar reservations about Brunetto's "By following your star/you cannot fail to reach a glorious port,/if I saw clearly in the happy life" (15:55–57). Star imagery carries a lot of weight in the *Commedia*. It is no accident that each of the *Commedia*'s three canticles, *Inferno, Purgatorio* and *Paradiso,* ends with the Italian word *stelle* ("stars"). In *Paradiso* you learn that stars and planets are animated by angelic presences whose job is to transmit God's divine light downward through the heavenly spheres and ultimately to earth, the heavens thus radiantly displaying the divine order in which the pilgrim is learning to find his bearings and his life's meaning. What does Brunetto mean by "star" here? How does the "glorious port" he advertises compare with the home to which Dante says he is being led (15:54; see also 1:112–29 where Virgil designates the pilgrim's ultimate destination as God's city)? How ultimately beneficial are Brunetto's paternal themes?

Ditto, given what we have learned about Fortuna, for Brunetto's first question to the pilgrim at lines 46–47: "What chance [fortuna] or fate is it that brings you here before your final hour?" What, compared to Virgil's description of Fortuna in canto 7, does Brunetto's use of the idea suggest about his worldview? How well would it nourish fledgling literary forays? Or mature ones?

The poet uses that other father figure, Virgil, as a counterpoint to nudge readers toward a more thoughtful appraisal of Brunetto. Visually, Virgil walks alongside Dante up on the dike. The pilgrim lowers his head to respond to Brunetto, whose contrapasso places him below on the sand. In contrast with Virgil, Brunetto has a lot to say. You imagine that he is the kind of mentor who takes pride in being regarded as a fountain of wise counsel. How far such pride would be justified I've questioned above. Virgil delivers only one line in response to the pilgrim's confident claims about his own mastery of the lesson about Fortuna: *Bene ascolta chi la nota* (15:99). The Hollanders translate this "He listens well who takes in what he hears." In this case I prefer Ciardi's "Well heeded is well heard," which better captures the contrast between Virgil's crisp moral directness and Brunetto's verbal abundance. I take Virgil to be telling Dante that it is a lot harder to live out a lesson about the vanity of worldly goods than it is to record it in your mental notebook. The pilgrim's two father figures employ very different styles of teaching, implying divergent understandings of the mentor's role and of what's good for the "son." What are the differences and who does better by his middle-aged child?

The poet accentuates this good-father question by dramatizing the pilgrim's contrasting responses to these two figures. Your students need to picture this three-person dance. The pilgrim honors Brunetto and all but ignores Virgil. Even when Brunetto asks about the guide's identity, the pilgrim skirts the question by referring to Virgil with the anonymous "he." (Wouldn't the writer in Brunetto relish the chance to meet the author of the *Aeneid*?) After a brief glance toward Virgil when he delivers his one line, the pilgrim quickly turns his attention back to Brunetto. Note the poet's edgy transition at this moment: "Nevertheless," which may express some criticism of the pilgrim's actions, as if Virgil's statement warrants more attention than it gets. The pilgrim, forgetting the source of the two lessons he claims in this canto to have learned — one about Fortuna and the other about how to handle troubling prophesies — makes clear which father spirit he prefers. This scene is that much more poignant when read in the context of the guide's departure from the pilgrim high on the Mount of Purgatory in canto 30 of *Purgatorio*. By that point, the pilgrim's tender sorrow over the loss of his guide, whom he calls "sweetest of fathers," marks significant maturation of his spirit.

The canto closes with a highly ambiguous quatrain, but only so, I'm claiming, if you confuse the pilgrim with the poet. Here's the Hollanders' translation of it:

> After he turned back he seemed like one
> who races for the green cloth on the plain
> beyond Verona. And he looked more the winner
> than the one who trails the field.

The double use of the verb *parve* ("seemed": the Hollanders unhelpfully translate the second occurrence as "looked") can express both the pilgrim's admiring view of Brunetto in the narrative past and the poet's implicit reservations about him now. The pilgrim thought him a winner, but that was only seeming, as the poet's scorching placement of him in hell suggests.

I hope these details and others you can draw from canto 15 support the case I'd like to make about the poet's intentions. Dante is never a single-valence poet. Throughout the *Commedia*, he is interested in the proportions of whole human lives. In *Inferno*, this produces pictures of how some uncontrolled human leanings can disfigure and finally destroy whole personalities. Brunetto's "scorched face" when Dante meets him is the very image of that disfigurement of a once-revered countenance. Then Dante would be concerned not as much with a character's specific sinful actions as with the disposition that dominates his life. Not just the act of suicide but the mind of a light denier. Not just a self-centered heresy but the fundamental denial of basic human communion. And so on.

I've been claiming that the theme in this canto is procreativity as applied to father figures. It judges how those in a paternal position discharged that responsibility. Allegorically, the canto would then deal with the parental faculty in every human soul, that part of us that responds to the call to subordinate our own interests to those of others depending on us for nurture or guidance. You have been in that position when you raised kids, guided any subordinate or follower, taught students in a high-school classroom, or acted as anyone's role model. It's a responsibility everyone has to assume at some time or other. A metaphorical sodomite fulfills his parental duty negligently, narcissistically, or otherwise detrimentally so as to produce nothing healthy from interaction with people whose welfare depends on him. This creates a desert where there should be flora.

For this interpretation to hang together, you'd expect the other desert runners in this canto to be in Brunetto's category: eminent people positioned in life to influence younger minds. And that, according to Brunetto, is what you do find: bands comprised entirely of "clerics or great and famous scholars." Brunetto mentions three particular companions, Francesco d'Accorso, Priscian, and Andrea de' Mozzi. All three were renowned in their day, and as with Brunetto, none is characterized as homosexual in any other source. So maybe specific homosexual acts are not the point, or not the main point. Dante may consider homosexuality as naturally correlated with unproductive parenthood, but on the logic here, it would be a supporting condition and not a necessary cause. You could take it away and still have something deplorable, and you could find it present in something good. Then you could find non-literal sodomites in this canto and unrepentant homosexuals in purgatory or paradise. (Repentant homosexuals are located with their heterosexual counterparts in *Purgatory* 26. Giving them equal treatment there must already set Dante apart from his contemporaries.)

In canto 16 Dante and Virgil come across three other distinguished Florentine sodomites who can be made to support the reasoning above, though you might not think so at first. In an article about these three, the Hollanders (1996) point out that "They are presented as being among the most admirable figures in Hell." They add, "it is a rare thing in the *Inferno* to find a moment in which the pilgrim, the poet, and the guide are all in absolute agreement, and certainly with respect to the human worth of sinners." If sodomites are condemned to this place in hell regardless of worth, doesn't that prove that homosexual acts are in fact decisive? At least in one respect, no. Regarding these three, guide and poet, unlike

Brunetto, seem to rival the pilgrim in admiration. The poet: "It pains me still, when I remember them" (15:12). The guide: "Now wait: to these one must show courtesy" (15:15). Your students could spend good time delving into reasons for preferring Iacopo Rusticucci, Guido Guerra, and Tegghiaio Aldobrandi to Brunetto. They might well decide that these were good father spirits. As influential political figures, they nurtured the city-state of Florence. According to the commentaries, they discharged that responsibility with great and benevolent effectiveness. Though they share Brunetto's position in hell, they occupy something more like a pleasant meadow in the mind of the poet. Here then is a place where the poet's evaluation may not be strictly congruent with his God's. I see this as a splendidly interesting complication. Your students might well conclude that to Dante the fact of homosexuality, though it does carry weight, is not the only charge that counts. Sometimes, as with Cato, God's judgments introduce complications; sometimes, as here, the poet's do. One thing seems clear to me from the varying character judgments of pilgrim, guide, poet, and God: a simple one-dimensional condemnation of homosexuality won't explain the data. This canto is at least more complicated than that. If your students can devise an explanation that does justice to the data, in detail, they will certainly surpass this teacher, and maybe you, too. That will be a moment worth cultivating.

I realize that all of this argument may finally be wish-fulfilling whitewash, and Dante may just be hewing to the medieval Catholic line on homosexuality. But I am persuaded by the details in this canto and by his treatment of other sins in *Inferno* to discover an independent-minded Dante here and on many other subjects. That said, I have a lot of personal ambivalence about canto 15. Even if you are convinced by my argument above, you are still left with a poet who pins a scarlet letter on his famous mentor, knowing that whatever his intention, most readers will take the sodomy charge literally. If Dante wanted to stake out a non-orthodox Christian perspective on homosexuality, he sure didn't do so very clearly. You have to work hard to arrive at that interpretation, though I do think careful reading will lead you there. If that wasn't what he wanted, then I have to accept that very great writers can take abhorrent positions. That's hard because I expect my literary greats to be sages too, especially in a poem that puts such a premium on better understanding of the human situation.

Exercises for Canto 10

THEMES AND ISSUES

1. Poet versus pilgrim and/or guide: how does the poet distance himself from the pilgrim's initially cowering behavior toward Farinata and from the

guide's respectful one? What specific passages from the text lead you to your answer to this question? What attitudes toward this striking character does the poet want his readers to share?

2. How is the general contrapasso for Epicurean heretics appropriate to their sin? Retributively? Allegorically, if false belief is another feature of the potentials inherent in the human soul? What details from the text justify your interpretation?

3. Is there a theme that unifies this canto? A strong answer to this question can be measured by how many of the canto's details it brings under its interpretive umbrella. Are there, as in other cantos, repeated words, phrases, or ideas to which your students can point to support their claims?

4. What figures of speech, particularly similes and allusions, shed light on the poet's attitudes toward the figures in this canto? Specifically, how does Dante use the allusion to Jesus's empty tomb (if it is an allusion) to illuminate by contrast his portrait of Farinata and the Epicureans?

5. To a Christian, what hinges on the belief in the soul's immortality that would justify creating a special category of sin for unbelievers? What is the relation between the lack of this belief and factionalism? Pride? A distorted sense of time?

6. How does this canto contribute to readers' understanding of Dante the poet's attitude toward pagan antiquity? (Note that pagans in limbo and Epicureans here occupy similar structural positions. Each group is situated at the doorstep of, but clearly outside, one of Dante's three major sinful domains, violence here and incontinence there. Neither group seems to fit neatly into Dante's overall scheme.) A good answer might begin by attending to lines 101–102: "for us, the mighty Ruler's light still shines." Does this canto contradict the depiction of limbo? If not, what specific distinctions, especially regarding sins of intellect, should be drawn between the other pagans in canto 4 and the Epicureans here?

Research

1. Among his many probable references to the Epicureans in the New Testament, St. Paul in his First Letter to the Corinthians famously states the following:

> What do I gain if, humanly speaking, I fought with beasts
> at Ephesus? If the dead are not raised, "Let us eat and drink,
> for tomorrow we die." (ESV 1 Corinthians 15:32)

Have your students, possibly in two different groups, read up on the historical Epicureans and Paul's biblical comments about them. You could raise many stimulating questions from this research, some of them a little inflammatory. The overarching one would obviously address the accuracy and defensibility of Paul's position. I would encourage you not to shy away from lighting little fires like this one in your classroom. My religiously conservative students often proved more than ready to address questions like this one with energy and fair-mindedness.

2. Have them look into Florentine politics in the thirteenth and early fourteenth centuries. What does a studied knowledge of Guelph and Ghibelline strife during this period add to the weight and poignancy of this canto, and to the entire *Inferno*?

Extension

What is wrong with substituting a part for the whole? Can your students cite real-world instances in which this all-too-human tendency led to destructive consequences?

Exercises for Canto 13

CLOSE READING

1. Reminding your students about the close relation between a canto's description of place and the sin positioned there, have them look closely at the Italian for the first three tercets. What are the implications of the anaphoric repetition of "non" as a line and canto opener for the sin of suicide?
2. How do Pier's first words characterize him? What about his shifts in tone and style of speech from painfully defensive as his twig is broken to proudly and elegantly insistent on his status and mistreatment at court to objectively succinct in explaining how souls take root in the wood of suicides? Dante in effect gives him three voices. How are those voices related to one another and to his present condition? Are there distinctions to be made in quality of character among these three Piers? One further implication of Pier's characterization: to Dante, the temple of God can have multiple rooms. All of *Inferno* testifies to this idea. You might want to make something of that with your students.
3. If the poet intends for readers to hear in Pier's proud reference to holding "both keys to Frederick's heart" (58–59) an allusion to Saint Peter and his

keys to the gates of heaven, to what end? It is no doubt significant that Pier means Peter in Italian. Two contrasting Peters. How would that contrast sharpen the characterization of Pier and help to explain what led to his suicide? A little biblical research could be beneficial here. line 62 —"So faithful was I to that glorious office"— might be relevant to these questions. It does not seem accidental that Pier uses religiously charged language here to describe his secular allegiance.

4. Note the poet's phrasing in line 25—*Cred'io ch'ei credette ch'io credesse*—which unmistakably reflects Pier's style of speech when he's in courtly mode. What is the point of this echo, so unlike the poet's normal narrative voice? According to one critic (Spitzer 1942), the line serves to indicate the pilgrim's confused state of mind at this point in his journey and to anticipate the note of disharmony that will pervade the whole canto. Your students might want to disagree with this interpretation. Unlike canto 5 where the pilgrim fell into Francesca's speech patterns in his own directly quoted speech, this line is delivered in present tense from the perspective of the poet who is stating what he now thinks. So I wonder, not too confidently, whether Dante is not parodying Pier here, in subtle criticism of a pretentious style of speech that reflects a mind gone far astray. It's at least a good question.

5. Here's a question about interpreting a detail at the end of this canto that has always puzzled me. Why, according to the anonymous suicide, would Florence have to suffer for replacing John the Baptist with Mars as its patron spirit? In a Christian poem, that seems counterintuitive. No commentary I've read yet has offered a very satisfying answer.

THEMES AND ISSUES

1. Under the ongoing problem of how to regard the damned, what kind of emotional response does the poet call for in this troubling canto? Is this a place where your students should see some distance between the poet and the pilgrim, who feels strong pity for Pier and who goes out of his way to make a kindly gesture toward the Florentine suicide? The pilgrim's behavior here is a far cry from how he handled the shade of Filippo Argenti a few cantos ago. Are the pilgrim's sympathies here a sign of maturation? Regression? And then more generally, what would your students endorse as a decent kind of emotional response to someone's suicide? Are there differences between how Christians and non-Christians would answer this question? Some of your students may want to separate the act from the person, which seems to be appropriate, or even essential,

to a humane way of wrestling with this question. Only note that Dante doesn't really allow his readers that distinction. In his Pier, there is little difference between the person and the act. Had there been, some kind of repentant better direction might have opened up for him. That's what it means to say that Pier has the mind of a suicide. There might be other voices in him, but they will ultimately be drowned out by the wailing of the Harpies. If this line of interpretation holds water, Dante's handling of this problem in a canto about suicide really might stir up student thinking.

2.   Here's another way to structure the contrapasso question. Think of how lexicographers construct definitions. A standard two-step method used in scientific taxonomy situates an item in a class and then cites its differentia, the qualities that distinguish it from other members of that class. So a table is a piece of furniture (class) with a horizontal top capable of supporting tankards of beer (differentia). (Or try a definition joke like Ambrose Bierce's sardonic "Love: a temporary insanity curable by marriage.") In cantos like this one with individualized sinners, Dante uses something like this method. He locates a particular sinner in a genus chiefly by placing him in the suffering-fraught setting of a canto that all such sinners share. Then he uses what the individuated shade does and says in the canto to differentiate him from others who share the genus. Thus he shows how a certain negative potential in all humans has deformed the soul of a particular human being. Both dimensions operating together create some of the most affecting episodes in *Inferno*. Ask your students to generalize as comprehensively as possible about the character of Pier delle Vigne as the pilgrim finds him in the wood of suicides. Good answers will take into account as many details as possible from Pier's physical situation as a tree, what we learn about his former life on earth, and what kind of spirit his words reveal him to be now. They might suggest a lot about what leads to the act of suicide, as Dante understands it.

RESEARCH

1.   Is a noble suicide possible? One way to approach this question is through cultural history. Have your students look up attitudes toward suicide in other cultures and times. What differences do they find? How have other cultures justified their beliefs about suicide?

2.   Have them research Cato the Younger. On what grounds would Dante distinguish him as a suicide from Pier delle Vigne? Or as a great pagan from Socrates and others? As a contemporary aside, you might ask some

students with political interests to look into the basis for the name of that influential contemporary think tank, the Cato Institute.

3. Have them find out what roles the Harpies play in classical mythology, with a special emphasis on Virgil's *Aeneid*, Dante's second-most-alluded-to text. As before, you can build on the literal/allegorical distinction. Allegorically, if the Harpies embody some feature or potential of the human makeup, what would it be? Good answers would have to be consistent with the Harpies' roles in the *Aeneid* as spoilers of the feast and prophets of disaster as well as in this canto as creatures whose wounds to suffering spirits "give pain and to that pain a mouth." That is, they both cause pain and provide a bloody outlet for its expression. In that way they are causally connected to the act of suicide. What propensity of the human psyche do these qualities describe?

Exercises for Canto 15

APPLICATIONS

More than most, this canto begs for topical treatment. Here are two ways to accomplish that:

1. The father question intra-canto: Who makes the good father spirit in this canto? What qualities would the pilgrim look for in one? What about the poet, at a hundred-canto remove from the dark wood? These are obviously inference questions requiring that good answers be explicitly grounded in the text.

    Then you can move beyond the text by questioning how far your students agree with the poet. This is a text-as-applied-to-life question requiring your students to pull up their own criteria for good literal or figurative fatherhood. Answers here still require supporting reasons, but they will naturally be colored by personal experience. This is an important question, don't you think, in an age obsessed with celebrity worship and plagued by weak or absentee fatherhood?

2. The more challenging gay question. I maintain right off that you will make this sensitive task harder if you try to take a disinterested position on it. Your job is to open up lines of inquiry and communication by being fair and by fostering respect for perspectives of all kinds without relinquishing the demand for good reasons. But you aren't required to be impartial. It's healthy for your students to have to deal with your biases in open discussion just as you do theirs. On topics like this, I found it helpful to arrange

the desks so that everyone, including the teacher, was on the same level and as far as possible in full view of everyone else. This signals that you are serious about real conversation and real listening. You will need to drop any idea that your opinion is privileged. Count on your students to assist you with this.

Still, it falls to you to provide structure to a conversation about Dante's ideas as applied to contemporary thinking and circumstances. It might be useful to bring up Lionel Trilling. In an essay about teaching literature, Trilling, a renowned American literature professor and critic, claimed that your ultimate question after finishing a piece of literature should be this: "Is it true? Is it true for me?" (Trilling 1967 "On the Teaching of Modern Literature") To respond regarding this canto, your students will need to agree on what "it," Dante's position on homosexuality, is as evidenced in the poem. If the arguments above have any validity, this may be no easy matter. But without at least provisional agreement, application questions won't make sense. Once they have that, Trilling's question will move them out of medieval Italy and into their own neighborhood. You may be digging open a water main there.

It will be up to you to figure out how to channel the outpouring. I certainly had my ups and downs trying to handle it. When under such pressure, it's good to keep some handy complicators in reserve. Here are two related ones that served me pretty well on this issue. First, the distinction between belief and action: isn't there a boundary somewhere between beliefs on which your students would take public action and their other beliefs? The important question is perhaps not how many of your students oppose gay marriage but how many would vote for a ballot initiative banning it. Pointing out this to them may introduce some beneficial tension into their thinking. This will probably be based in a second useful complication: conflicts of belief or values. Point out that their particular beliefs don't exist in a vacuum, though they are often encouraged to believe that they do. Suggest that such encouragement can act as an inducement to sentimentalism. Have them envision mental scales on which a given belief in particular circumstances has to be weighed against conflicting beliefs or values on the other side. The demand to give appropriate weight ought to be no respecter of political or religious affiliations. Liberal to conservative: don't you feel some conflict between your belief that gay marriage should be banned and the democratic principle of equal treatment under the law? Conservative to liberal: aren't your attempts to suppress religion-based opposition to homosexuality in public at odds with reasonable respect for traditions that have passed time's test and have gained the support of millions?

Dante the poet seems to me quite conflicted about how he feels about the men he categorizes as sodomites. He might share the orthodox rejection of homosexuality, but that is obviously tempered in some cases by other considerations. The three Florentine sodomites can inspire respect even from the poet. Reproducing that kind of conflict in the minds of your students is a lot of what an education should be about, academically or morally. They might begin to talk their way around some barriers.

6

That Foul Effigy of Fraud

CANTO 17

Geographical features as conspicuous as the cliff with a waterfall in this canto deserve your attention. As at any prominent discontinuity in the poem, here again you ought to ask the structure question. Construct it out of some glaringly counterintuitive contrast between sins above and below this cliff, in upper and lower hell, from the circles of incontinence or violence on the one hand and fraud on the other. On what logic is, say, false counsel (cantos 26 and 27) worse than murder (canto 12)?

Beginning in canto 17, Dante implicitly lays out his answer to such questions. It takes him a while. He requires half of *Inferno* to complete a lengthy taxonomy of the two sprawling circles of fraud. But Virgil has already explicitly addressed the classification of fraud in his canto 11 survey: "since the vice of fraud is man's alone,/ it more displeases God, and thus the fraudulent/ are lower down, assailed by greater pain" (11:25–27). Recall my outline in chapter 4 of the three categories of sin. Other species can be incontinent or violent, but only humans employ intellectual deceit in the service of harming others. While incontinence entails corrupted appetites and violence corrupted appetites and emotions, only fraud perverts all three parts of the soul including the intellect, that essentially human third dimension. This strongly distinguishes sins of the spotted beast in canto 1 from those of the lion (violence) and the she-wolf (incontinence). Virgil then divides fraud into two subcategories according to whether it is used against those with whom one has a special bond of trust. The latter cases of compound fraud are punished in the ninth circle of *Inferno* beginning in canto 31. Simple fraud is housed in Malebolge, a series of concentric ditches hacked into a rock wall. Together, these constitute circle eight, which, after being deposited at the waterfall's bottom in canto 17, Dante and Virgil begin to negotiate.

At this threshold, Dante the poet uses bold strokes to set fraud apart and define its general nature. Topographically, he locates lower hell at the bottom of a waterfall pouring over a towering cliff. Emblematically, he posts near the waterfall a winged monster, huge, intimidating, and distinctively configured. So categorically discontinuous are the violent in circle seven from the fraudulent in eight that the only way down the cliff is to fly on the monster's back. That creature, Geryon, "this worst of brutes" (17:23), "that foul effigy of fraud" (17:7) may be the most elaborately worked image in *Inferno*. Because he represents qualities that the many dwellers in lower hell share, he must carry a lot of figurative weight.

The first thing to note is Geryon's size; to the pilgrim he looms terrifyingly large. This squares with the magnitude of the offense he represents. The poet describes his composition in three segments: a hairy lion's body with a scorpion's poisoned tail attached, both belied in front by the face "of a righteous man,/ benevolent in countenance" (17:10–11). Obviously, Geryon shares some beastliness with monsters in previous circles. As Dante learns from Virgil before passing through the gates of hell in canto 3, all those he will see inside "have lost the good of the intellect" (3:18). Since Virgil emphasizes the species-defining weight of intellect in canto 11, you might conclude that all those punished in hell lack to some degree that faculty which makes us human. Hence Dante's use of emblematic non-human monsters like Cerberus, the Minotaur, and now Geryon. But Geryon differs in kind from previous monsters in exhibiting a deceptively guileless human face. What sets fraud apart is not lack of intellect, but its perverted use.

Throughout the incontinent and violent sections of hell, human defilement was pretty blatant. Francesca's windy lustiness flaunted itself even in hell, and on earth the violent had committed Minotaur-like acts of overtly aggressive malice against God, self, or neighbor. But with the figure of Geryon, Dante introduces the theme of deceit. Below the cliff are punished sins (represented by the leopard in canto 1) that make use of the human ability to "smile and smile and be a villain." As Hamlet recognizes, an innocent-looking face can sugar over the most poisonous of intentions. So ask your students how the three parts of Geryon as described at the beginning of canto 17 represent fraudulent action generally. (An example: I read somewhere an interpretation of Geryon's make-up as a template for human sting operations: the innocent face of the predator lures the victim in, his colorfully embroidered coat dazzles the victim as the ruse develops, and finally the "envenomed tip" of the tail lashes around to deliver the painful outcome.) It's a pretty arresting place for your students to exercise their powers.

At one point in his description of Geryon, Dante the poet once again steps out of narrative mode to address the reader directly. In doing so, he reiterates, if testimony were needed, that his *Commedia* is not just concerned with otherworldly issues. In describing the way Geryon swims up to the top of the waterfall at Virgil's signal, the poet expresses in present tense his retrospective attitude toward this event:

> To a truth that bears the face of falsehood
> a man should seal his lips if he is able,
> for it might shame him, through no fault of his.
>
> But here I can't be silent. And by the strains
> of this Comedy—so may they soon succeed
> in finding favor—I swear to you, reader,
>
> That I saw come swimming up
> through that dense and murky air a shape
> to cause amazement in the stoutest heart,
>
> A shape most like a man's who, having plunged
> to loose the anchor caught fast in a reef
> or something other hidden in the sea, now rises,
> reaching upward and drawing in his feet. (16:124–36)

Critics have had a lot to say about this puzzling passage. One question they raise deals with the nature and function of fictional art as Dante sees it. Among other intentions, maybe Dante is using this passage to worry out the difference between writing a narrative poem like the *Commedia* and committing acts of fraud. In one sense at least, can't all fiction be located in Geryon's huge shadow? That is, don't fictional narratives intend to embody truths "that bear the face of falsehood" (literally *menzogna*: a lie)? False faces that convey readers to truths veiled behind? As with Geryon? Isn't the *Commedia*, then, a piece of fraud? The *Commedia*'s many such self-referential moments teach you, I think, that Dante spends a lot of time worrying about how this work should be classified. Which only makes sense in a poem so preoccupied itself with classifications.

This question is complicated by the acknowledged fact that the *Commedia* is allegorical, allegory being the literary form that sharply and consistently distinguishes a figurative surface story from the much more important set of truthful ideas that it represents. If any kind of literature belongs in the truth-with-the-face-of-a-lie category, allegory does. In the *Commedia*, I remind you, Dante is trying to create a different kind of allegory, one in which there is not such a strong separation between the literal and figurative levels, between surface appearance and underlying truth. In a previous work, the *Convivio*, Dante famously calls allegorical poetry a beautiful lie, using the same word for lie, *menzogna*, as in the passage above. There he seemed happy with the literary lie. More worried here, he swears by the poem itself that what he experienced was literally as well as figuratively true. He probably intends this oath to take you aback. How can his swearing in present tense to the truth of encountering a mythological beast be taken seriously? Maybe he is prompting you to wonder whether there is some other sense in which what he claims can be true. If so, this might be his way of fending off the charge of fraud. It anyway seems clear that Dante is trying to carve out for his poem a special non-fraudulent category distinguishing it from other allegories and a lot of other literature.

I have to admit that the passage above generates puzzles I can't begin to solve with any confidence. But I do know that you can use it to raise some good questions. What is the difference between fraud and fictional literature? Perhaps some literature is fraudulent. What then distinguishes fraudulent literature from a better kind? More specifically, how does the *Commedia* evade the charge of fraud?

Finally, consider Geryon narratively. Under Virgil's guidance, the pilgrim's education entails not just understanding but appropriate action. How does he teach the pilgrim to deal with fraud in this imposing form? Here it helps to realize how frequently in *Inferno* Virgil prods his reluctant charge to, in effect, take a closer look for himself. Before Geryon rises in canto 17, you hear it again. Virgil urges Dante to "go over and examine" the usurers "so that nothing in this circle escape your understanding." To Virgil, apparently, you can't get a proper infernal education from a distance. It requires direct experience—as unflinching an examination at close quarters as the pilgrim can muster. The pilgrim's developing ability to make close approaches seems to be every bit as important in his education as what he sees when he gets there. Approaching the usurers is not too daunting a prospect, but Geryon is another story. The prospect of being ferried down to lower hell on his hairy back terrifies the pilgrim, as the poet emphasizes repeatedly in the scene. Only Virgil's prompting to be "strong and resolute" shames Dante into climbing aboard. They key image in the passage is Virgil's, however, when he characterizes the descent on the beast as *scale*, stairs. This prefigures a yet more dramatic use of the same image to express a similar notion at the end of *Inferno*. To me, the idea implied here is one of the most profound in the poem. The close encounter with the negative potentials that all humans share apparently acts as a vehicle for forward, and ultimately, upward movement. Without the courage to climb those stairs, it seems, the journey of our life founders.

Exercises

CLOSE READING

1. What are the implications of the cliff/waterfall imagery connecting the last of the violent above with the first of the fraudulent below?
2. Ditto for the elaborate description of Geryon, as the announced emblem of fraud (17:1–27; 91–136). What must all the fraudulent in the last half

of *Inferno* have in common if Geryon is their common emblem? As always for long descriptions, the more details brought to bear on an interpretive claim, the stronger the claim.

3. How to interpret the poet's sworn testimony to seeing the mythical beast Geryon swim up from below? Dante is so insistent about this that he uses the *Commedia* itself as collateral.

4. The image of stairs (17:82) as applied to Geryon and what it implies about proper action when the terrible manifestation of human evil threatens to arrest your progress on the journey.

THEMES AND ISSUES

1. Geryon's emblematic function is to represent the genus of fraud. What is the difference between fraudulent acts and the writing of the *Commedia*? Between fraudulent fictional literature and its opposite?

2. Between different kinds of allegory? Dante scholars have worked this ground pretty thoroughly. In fact Robert Hollander has devoted an entire book to the two kinds of allegory in Dante's work. But it might suffice to ask your students what might distinguish the *Commedia* from other allegories. If they haven't read other allegories, just lay out for them a brief summary of how, say, *The Pilgrim's Progress* works. They'll see some telling contrasts right away. How far do those contrasts help exonerate the author of the *Commedia* on the question of fraud?

3. What do the actions of guide and pilgrim regarding Geryon imply about the way to deal with the negative possibilities in human nature. How far do you think the poet intends for the implication here to be applied universally in *Inferno*?

APPLICATIONS

In Kurt Vonnegut's (2006) *Cat's Cradle*, when one character claims "I'm not a drug salesman. I'm a writer," a second replies, "What makes you think a writer isn't a drug salesman?" (153). Use the Vonnegut quote to set up the distinction between a writer at his best and a writer as drug salesman. The latter category seems consonant with what Dante might consider fraudulent writing. Once your students have fleshed out this contrast in discussion, you can find a lot of interesting ways to develop it. Stage a set of oral book reviews in which students singly or in groups compare in some detail two books they have read using this distinction. It might be interesting to have them choose, as far as possible, books they have read for your class. Have them quote from the works they are reviewing to make their points.

7

A Miscellany of Fraud

CANTOS 18–25

If you have made use in class of even a fraction of the suggestions above, you may be feeling time's chariot pressing you behind. Unlike a lucky friend of mine who teaches a semester-long Dante class at a prep school in Baltimore, you probably can't afford to spend as much time on the last half of *Inferno* as you have on the first. The remarkably dense texture of the *Commedia* does have its classroom liabilities. So maybe you are looking for a rationale to quicken the pace.

For my classes, I found that I could provide one, if anywhere, for cantos 18 through 25. These act as an introduction to fraud, that uniquely human kind of shortcoming. The *Inferno* makes fraud seem like the most pervasive of human sins, since it takes Dante and Virgil the entire second half of *Inferno* to cover all its subcategories. Beginning with canto 18 Dante gives readers a long time to ponder the forms fraud can take. It was always hard for me to sustain concentration, my students' or my own, over fraud's seventeen-canto spread. I found myself eager to get to *Inferno* 26, which touches off a memorable set of encounters building to a climax (with perhaps an eventual "anti") by the end. One reason for that eagerness was the lack of much development of particular human cases of fraud in cantos 18 to 25. You get interesting subcategories of simple fraud whose members suffer suitably agonizing contrapassos. You find quite a bit of interaction between pilgrim and guide, which continues to mark the slow maturation of the pilgrim. And you encounter some intriguing digressions and shifts of tone. But you don't find much of what I value most in *Inferno*: conversation-spiced illustrations of how particular types of sin color individual lives. So I propose to deal with these cantos in one chapter by brief development of a few of the prominent, interesting, or puzzling elements in them.

Canto 19: Simony

Among other things, this canto exhibits Dante's love of wordplay, especially when it's biblically grounded. Take a look at the term for the transgression this canto deals with: simony. It refers to the buying and selling of ecclesiastical favors, implicating in Dante's day various church figures who used their position to enrich themselves and their supporters. Nothing too surprising here. The morally corrupt lives of the well-placed and powerful. Ho-hum.

But using his key term like a surgeon, Dante opens up for inspection the putrid body of the Catholic church in his day, almost rubbing your nose in its decay. "Simony" alludes to a biblical passage in which Simon Magus tries to buy the power to impart the Spirit of God (ESV Acts 8:9–25). Simon Peter's answer: "May your silver perish with you, because you thought you could obtain the gift of God with money! You have neither part nor lot in this matter, for your heart is not right before God" (Acts 8:20–21). Here are two Simons expressing two sharply different attitudes about "the gift of God." Simon Peter, on whom the papacy was founded, reprimands Simon Magus, whose take on the relation between money and religious power many subsequent popes seem to have inherited. In hastening to sift out the implications of this contrast, you may find that you've been handed a tool for evaluating any historical pope along one important dimension. Which Simon did he follow? Peter and some exceptional popes on one end of the continuum; Simon Magus and his numerous papal ilk on the other. So here's a nice little poetic gambit: Dante uses a chance piece of name association to craft a pretty sharp-edged evaluative device. The result is a greater sense of order in the poem. (Understatement: Dante's God has a penchant for morally intelligible order.)

But as canto 19 makes clear, Dante uses the notion of simony primarily as a means of lambasting papal corruption in his own day. This canto reserves particularly strong contempt for Boniface VIII, who was notorious for avaricious political and financial maneuvering. In Dante's reference to him here, the stench of decay, personal and institutional, is palpable. Dante casts Boniface as, if not the antichrist, at least one of his closest associates, with Nicholas III, the speaking simoniac in this canto, not far behind. Inherent in Dante's criticism of contemporary popes are his concerns about the assumption of political power by the church in the Italy of his day. The *Commedia* repeatedly expresses the poet's opposition to any form of religious control of political institutions.

As before, I'm backing the idea that the contrapasso here configures the state of being at death of the tribe of Simon Magus. There must be something wrong side up about what popes like Nicholas and Boniface made of themselves. Some critics have noted in this context that Simon Peter was crucified upside down.

There might be some profitable contrast there. In interpreting the imagery of fire, you might consider the possibly ironic relation between the flames licking the surface of Nicholas's feet and the fire of the Holy Spirit that descends upon the disciples and other believers on the day of Pentecost, reported in Acts 2:1–31. For a canto constructed out of its governing term's biblical foundation, such further scriptural references seem entirely appropriate.

Canto 20 Digression: Mantua's Founding

What about Virgil's long digression on the founding of his hometown, Mantua (*Inferno* 20:52–99)? How would a poet of Dante's stature justify this passage, nearly half a canto in length, discussing facts so loosely related to his narrative? How will it profit readers trying to understand the pilgrim's journey to ponder the hydrography of a region of northern Italy? It's puzzling that the poem compels you to raise this question without providing much immediate context in which to answer it. All that geographical detail just comes out of nowhere, bearing little obvious relation to Mantua or to the seer Manto who gave it her name. But under the premise that in great literature everything works, you might set your students to work examining the function of this piece of apparently digressive material in the poem.

Though I'm not at all sure what they will find, I do have an approach to recommend. Try to tease a context out of the rest of the *Commedia*. You do this by looking for framing patterns, in this case for other places in the poem where the imagery of flowing water might provide some basis for understanding what's behind this canto's lengthy tangent. Your students won't really be reading the *Commedia* well until they learn to recognize its patterns.

Two other sets of watery images in the *Commedia* come to mind. The description of the Old Man of Crete in *Inferno* 14 uses falling water as a means to discuss the sources and history of human suffering. Starting with an Edenic golden age on Mt. Ida in Crete, human tears (what causes those tears?) create the flow that cleaves the Old Man's body and ultimately feed the rivers of hell. Right below the golden head, falling teardrops cuts a channel through the silver, brass, and iron sections of that huge physique. As often before, Dante turns a classical paradigm to Christian uses here. He uses the declining ages of man from Greek mythology to establish a causality connecting some post-Eden fissure in human nature to the geography of hell. Any guesses about what that flaw might be?

Readers who know the rest of the *Commedia* might also want to include here the description of the river Lethe at the top of the Mount of Purgatory. If, as many scholars believe, Lethe's is the stream bed by which Virgil and Dante ascend toward purgatory at the end of *Inferno*, then that river connects the earthly paradise high on the mountain (see *Purgatorio* 28) to the icy depths of hell (see *Inferno* 34:127–39). Again the water's downward movement maps an arc of human decline. Maybe *the* arc. An original pure and innocent state of nature includes a stream that eventually flows down to the ultimate agony of alienation from the source of goodness and light at hell's dark bottom. Consistent with the Greek in which Lethe means forgetfulness, drinking from that river in Dante's earthly paradise erases all memory of one's sins. From there Lethe runs, say the Hollanders, "down into hell filled with the sins now forgotten by all who have purged themselves of them." (*Purgatorio* 28:131-32) Those landing on the shores of the Lethe-fed Acheron in *Inferno* 3 are thus condemned to remember their sins forever. They only get to experience Lethe downstream, after it has become polluted. Falling water is thus Dante's chosen vehicle for mapping biblical history in the fall of man.

You can use these two sets of images to analyze the Manto passage along similar lines. Begin with the "thousand" clear springs that feed pristine Lake Benaco, high in the Italian Alps. Include in this picture the imagery of sanctity: a small island or promontory where stands a chapel on a point at which three church dioceses converge. Then trace the flow of the river Mincio from Benaco, "through green pastures" until it soon levels off to make a swamp in the middle of which Manto, the now hideously deformed diviner whom Virgil identifies for Dante in canto 20, made her home. Falling water leads to a polluted world below that naturally fosters beings like Manto (Her sin? Maybe something close to classical hubris: the twistedly prideful tendency to evoke comparison with the divine—in her case by claiming to know the future).

Obviously, the Mantua materials move in pretty close step with the other two passages, but with one notable divergence: Virgil himself. Apparently the fallen world can spawn not just perverted mantic arts but also true artistic mastery. The *Commedia* itself, born out of the anguish of separation from the light in a dark wood, reinforces this point. The idea also coheres, for example, with Virgil's canto 11 explanation of the logic of placement of the usurers: "By toil and nature, if you remember Genesis, near the beginning, it is man's lot to earn his bread and prosper" (11:106–08, see also Genesis 3:19). Notice that the word that Hollander translates as toil is *l'arte* in the Italian. So artistic creativity, among other kinds of work, will have to arise from the interaction between human effort and a harsh post-Edenic natural world. For good reasons, great books commonly emerge from the fetid swamp, not some crystalline lake on high. You might infer that a Christian writer like Dante is a little ambivalent about the fallen world. The Manto passage would then constitute one means of expressing that ambivalence.

This raises good questions about the conditions for the production of great art. Engaging projects investigating the lives of great artists suggest themselves here. You could easily stack the deck: Whence Dostoevsky's novels? Dickenson's poetry? Van Gogh's painting? Beethoven's symphonies? John Stuart Mill's philosophical writings? Can any plausible generalization be framed here?

Canto 24: The Epic Simile, Maximized

One of the most elaborate similes in the *Commedia* opens canto 24 (1–21). A figure of speech this complex has naturally spawned a variety of readings. The Hollanders' helpful note for these lines outlines the two most common lines of interpretation:

1. Virgil's frown (hoarfrost) melts and he once again encourages Dante (the humble wretch), who eventually will, having completed the journey, feed us (his sheep) on the pages of the poem.
2. The devils' deception (hoarfrost), in the form of an incorrect presentation of the terrain, discourages Virgil (the wretch), who finally reads the signs right and will lead Dante (his sheep) to pasture.

Each approach has its merits and shortcomings. The first accords better with the verbal correspondences in the first part of the simile but strains a bit, I think, to make readers the sheep that Dante will drive to pasture. The second makes better sense of that element, but not of Virgil's face, which, like the changing face of the world, immediately and not eventually encourages the pilgrim to move forward.

But what warrants here such artistic extravagance for initiating a canto about hypocrisy and thievery? The Hollanders' claim that it serves to "knit the narrative back together" may be apt, but it hardly seems to justify the scope of this simile. Is there anything that makes it appropriate to the sixth bolgia theme of hypocrisy? Do you see anything in it that conceptually knits together hypocrisy and thievery?

Some Humor Sprinkled in

Here's a backhanded way to introduce the topic of humor in the *Inferno*. (That's right; I am claiming humor.) Get hold of Gustave Dore's engraving of Dante's face or maybe Botticelli's painting of him. Both are easy to find on the web, and both cast him as the severest and least sympathetic of judges. A little investigation will show you that this assessment is common in Dante portraiture. Artists rarely offer much to soften his features. Ask your students, once they have read up through canto 25, how well such portraits correspond to their developing sense of the poet behind the poem. What does the image of Dante the harsh judge of fallen mankind leave out? Would a smiling Dante ever make sense? Get them to entertain the possibility of a more human Dante, one with a sense of humor, for whom evidence isn't hard to find, particularly in these cantos. Here are a few instances of it:

1. Isn't there something familiarly funny about the contrapasso of the flatterers in canto 18, where those who achieved their malicious ends by flattery are immersed in and snorting excrement? Why does that instantly seem so appropriate? I wonder if there has ever been a culture that didn't associate some nasty oral effluents with posterior ones. Your students won't have to look far to find contemporary English expressions that make this connection. People everywhere seem to take some amusement in this means of deriding deceptive speech.

2. Consider Nicholas's line at canto 19:53–54: "Is that you already, are you here already, Boniface?" Might not Italians living under the corruption of Boniface's power hungry papacy snicker a little, perhaps up their sleeve, at the suggestion of Boniface soon to be squashed upside down atop other corrupt ecclesiastics in a rock hole deep in hell? It's the kind of image that gets brought up after a few beers at the local tavern where underlings are lightening the frustrations of subordination. We relish opportunities to laugh at our superiors, especially corrupt or tyrannical ones.

3. Most obviously, take a look at the behavior of the Malebranche devils in cantos 21 to 23. It's farce, slapstick, vaudeville to the coarsest of music. The demons compete boastfully with one another, are called to muster by an obscenely preposterous signal code, are easily deceived by a sinner, and fall to boisterous quarreling with one another when the sinner escapes. Two of the main squabblers then tumble into the pitch to be "cooked to a crust." Most memorably ridiculous, other than the "outlandish fanfare" of the flatulent trumpet call, might be the image of pilgrim and guide hesitantly setting off "escorted by ten demons." The poet uses a four tercet buildup to highlight that phrase. These cantos generally feature the poem's longest sustained foray into the comic mode.

Your students will no doubt find something to smile at in other passages in these cantos. This evidence raises two kinds of questions. The first concerns the structure of the text. What ends does the humor serve in the context of what Dante is trying to accomplish in the poem? The assumptions behind Shakespeare's penchant for emotional balance—stretches of comedy even toward the end of tragedy, as in *Hamlet*—might be apposite here. Unrelieved misfortune is hard for an audience to bear. The second question concerns the poet himself. Why would the cultivation of a less-severe image of himself serve the poet's interests in the poem? Here I'd remind you of my general drift in these chapters—that Dante's God has constructed not nearly so draconian a moral universe as a first glance would suggest. The poet presses you hard to reconsider your skepticism about the "Primal Love" engraved above the gates of hell in canto 3.

Since for all the items in this chapter I've framed some questions that might be useful for you, I'll not add any more here. As always, my hope is to provide you some backdrop against which to develop your own good questions.

8

Tongues

CANTO 26

To me, this is the most intriguing canto in *Inferno*. After all, it features Ulysses, one of the two greatest fictional heroes ever created, at least if you're a Grecophile. ("Ulysses" is the Latinization of the Greek "Odysseus.") He is the protagonist of Homer's *Odyssey*, and at least implicitly of many subsequent adaptations. W. B. Stanford's (2000) great critical work *The Ulysses Theme*, traces his literary progeny, right up through Joyce's *Ulysses*. Successful recent adaptations include the novel *Cold Mountain* and the film *Oh Brother, Where Art Thou?* Stanford develops strong reasons why Odysseus has proved a much more adaptable literary figure to subsequent artists than Achilles (or any other classical figure).

The best general approach to interpreting canto 26 might focus on Ulysses as the archetypal journeyer. One good way to acquaint yourself with this terrain is to read John Freccero's preface to the Robert Pinsky (1993) edition of *Inferno*. It's short, fairly accessible and full of the interpretive depth you'd expect from one of the preeminent English-speaking Dante scholars of the last half century. Among many valuable insights there, Freccero implies that comparative thinking will take you far in this canto. Again you will find parallels and contrasts doing a lot of work for the poet. Freccero's particular emphasis is on the journey motif. In light of the poem's first line, he naturally regards this theme as fundamental to *Inferno*. He discusses some of the similarities between Ulysses's journey as described in canto 26 and the pilgrim's as recounted in the whole *Commedia*: both move toward the Mount of Purgatory; both involve shipwreck, Ulysses's literally and Dante's figuratively in the poem's first canto; and both should be understood at more than one level. According to Freccero, "Ulysses was a traditional emblem in antiquity of the soul's journey, without a guide, to its celestial home." Substitute Dante for Ulysses in this quote, add a guide, and you have something like the *Commedia*, especially allegorically. But Freccero proceeds to show how Dante the poet sets up such parallels as a basis for differentiation. Ulysses' journey is tragic, ending in disaster for himself and his crew. Dante's is comedic, leading to paradise, where the pilgrim gains a direct perception of divine light. To Freccero, the presence or absence of a guide is at the heart of this difference. In Ulysses's speech to his men late in canto 26, Freccero hears "self-confidence . . . with its emphasis on a purely human rationality and no mention of the need for spiritual self-discipline or humility." Dante's Ulysses (like Homer's) would never conceive of the need for a guide. Pagans, unlike Christians, believe they can move forward and upward on their own. At least Dante seems to have drawn that conclusion.

With or without Freccero's help, you would do well to set aside a sizable chunk of classroom discussion time for distinguishing these two journeys. (Moving toward different ends? Serving dissimilar values, based on contrasting pictures of the world? Those ends and values conditioning different means, so that along the way the paths diverge in fundamental ways? Implying conflicting assumptions about the role that reason should play in our life's journey? Containing sharply contrasting approaches to the Mount of Purgatory? And so on.) There's a rich vein to tap here.

For literary and cultural history considered broadly, the most rewarding contrasts here might focus on the heroic idea. If a hero in traditional epic often embodies a culture's vision of human excellence, then a Ulysses, whose cardinal virtue was intelligence, points from the beginning to what is distinctive about classical Greek culture. Dante's characterization of him in canto 26 sets him sharply apart from the Christian hero of the *Commedia*. The poor pilgrim, though highly intelligent, (maybe *because* he's too adept philosophically) must develop different qualities to sustain his movement through hell and beyond. Judging by the pilgrim's progress, and at times the lack of it, what virtues is the poet stacking up against the classical ones? Insofar as the *Commedia* is meant to be a Christian epic, how does the poet distinguish a classical hero from a Christian one? This canto provides you with some of the poem's best material for addressing that question. Since something like that question was what first brought me to Dante, you can see why I lay so much weight on canto 26

It will help to offer your students some context: Homer's *Odyssey*. For maximum interpretive yield from canto 26, nothing can substitute for knowing that prototypical journey story. If I succeed in convincing you to teach the *Inferno*, perhaps you'll take the further step of inserting the *Odyssey* somewhere near the beginning of your course. It is an eminently teachable work. And to amend a famous quip, all of western literature is but a footnote to Homer. (I can't really defend this claim, of course, but I confess I do in part believe it.) Any good *Inferno* edition will point out that the details of Dante's depiction of Ulysses have no basis in Homer. Since few, if any, Europeans in Dante's time knew classical Greek, they could have no direct knowledge of the *Odyssey*. Dante certainly didn't. Nothing like the journey Dante gives Ulysses appears in the Homeric poems. The Ulysses you are getting in Dante's poem is a Christian version, at some distance from the Homeric original. To a Homerophile like me, the task of trying to measure that distance only makes this canto more interesting.

Stanford's book explains how Dante's conception of Ulysses may be implicit in the Homeric hero, but only from one side. Consider Odysseus' seminal attribute in the *Odyssey*: clever intelligence. By repeated instances of quick, on-his-feet thinking during his journey home, Odysseus finds a way to turn a variety of difficult situations to his advantage. Do you consider such cunning a virtue or a vice? The Greeks seemed to deem it the former, but many a later writer has wanted to explore its manipulative, opportunistic underbelly. This ambiguity accounts for much of this character's attraction for later artists. A Christian depiction like Dante's naturally emphasizes Ulysses' darker side.

Familiarity with the Homeric background would certainly deepen your students' understanding of Dante's characterization of Ulysses. Through reading about him in Homer, they can absorb this Greek essence in one of the best of ways: from character and action in a memorable story. Odysseus might come to epitomize for them why classical Greek culture still stands in such high regard. And by seeing firsthand the differences between Odysseus and Ulysses, they could get a better grip on how Dante's Christianity shapes his perspective.

That gives you three journeys to lay out for class discussion: those of Odysseus, Ulysses and the pilgrim. You might as well go ahead and include the obvious fourth: the journey of Virgil's Aeneas. Then you could trace the heroic ideal from Homer through Virgil to Dante. Though that prospect might seem dizzying, you'd be charting one of the richest of literary lineages. A real education lies there.

But these, I admit, are the urgings of a zealot. You certainly don't have to have studied all those epics to get started teaching Dante. There are many other angles of approach to this canto. One of the most prominent of them foregrounds questions about language. No careful reader will overlook the part effective speech plays in any of these journey narratives. For the Odysseus of the *Odyssey*, resourceful speech proves critical at several points to his progress toward Ithaka. His renowned wily intelligence expresses itself most vividly in his mastery of the rhetorician's art. He really knows how to size up an audience. The following famous passage from book 3 of the *Iliad* (Lombardo 1997) shows how integral to Odysseus' heroic identity is his way with words. Up on the tower by the Scaean gates of Troy, Helen is identifying the Greek warriors on the battlefield below to Priam, the venerable old king of Troy. Her pointing out of Odysseus prompts this famous remembrance from the Trojan hero Antenor:

Odysseus came here once before, on an embassy
For your sake along with Menelaus.
I entertained them courteously in the great hall
And learned each man's character and depth of mind.
Standing in a crowd of Trojans, Menelaus,
With his wide shoulders, was more prominent,
But when both were seated Odysseus was lordlier.
When it came time for each to speak in public
And weave a spell of wisdom with their words,
Menelaus spoke fluently enough, to the point
And very clearly, but briefly, since he is not
A man of many words. Being older, he spoke first.
Then Odysseus, the master strategist, rose quickly,
But just stood there, his eyes fixed on the ground.
He did not move his staff forward or backward
But held it steady. You would have thought him
A dull, surly lout without any wit. But when he
Opened his mouth and projected his voice
The words fell down like snowflakes in a blizzard.
No mortal could have vied with Odysseus then,
And we no longer held his looks against him.
(*Iliad* 3:220–40)

What marks the original version of this hero, then, is not so much physical strength, battlefield prowess, or personal charisma as verbal dexterity and the wisdom it expresses. His is a powerful mind communicated powerfully in words.

The *Inferno*'s treatment of Ulysses shows that this essential Greek trait, at least, has not been winnowed out of his character by Dante's time. There are a number of indications that Dante intends canto 26 to focus on the uses and misuses of language, especially by virtuosos like Ulysses. Contrapasso imagery, for one. Dante describes each flame in this bolgia as like a "tongue of fire" (89) "moving along the gullet of the trench" (40–41), suggesting that mouths and what comes out of them will be featured here. Lines 64 to 78 concern themselves with who is going to speak to the forked flame containing the spirits of Ulysses and Diomedes. The passage is dense with references to the act of speech and its vehicles: tongues and words. And when Ulysses sets going his memorable monologue, he seems proudest of the power of his speech to move aging crewmen to do his will. So much so that he recites from memory the whole speech for the pilgrim and guide, even though it led to disaster for all aboard his ship.

Both poet and pilgrim are characterized here by their attraction to verbal prowess. The pilgrim feels so strongly the appeal of what this bolgia contains that he at first almost falls into it. He is so anxious to hear Ulysses speak that he petitions Virgil with this passionate plea:

> If they can speak within those flames,
> I said, "I pray you, master, and I pray again—
> and may my prayer be a thousand strong—
>
> "do not forbid my lingering awhile
> until the twin-forked flame arrives.
> You see how eagerly I lean in its direction." (26:64–69)

It must seem to the pilgrim like the chance of a lifetime. The opportunity to hear this legendary master rhetorician is not to be missed, especially by someone who is in the process of staking his own claim to verbal excellence.

The poet leans forward too, even though he should know better. In literary fame lurks a potential danger, of which a Christian poet might be particularly well aware. Dante the poet illustrates what I mean through some comments he makes in present tense in cantos 25 and 26. In canto 25 the poet can't keep from some competitive gloating about the imaginative power of his verse:

> Let Lucan now fall silent where he tells
> of poor Sabellus and Nasidius
> and let him wait to hear what comes forth now!
>
> Let Ovid not speak of Cadmus and Arethusa,
> for if his poem turns him into a serpent
> and her into a fountain, I grudge it not,
>
> for never did he change two natures, face to face,
> in such a way that both their forms
> were quite so quick exchanging substance. (25:94–102)

These lines would be right at home in a Homeric battle scene, in which boasting over bested foes is the norm. Here they signal poetic combat at the highest level, with Dante emerging as the clear winner, at least in his own eyes. However justified the poet's claims are here, it is hard to see these as Christian sentiments. You'd think the poet's trip to heaven would have gotten him past this kind of chest thumping, but perhaps the point is fame's power to turn even a head keenly aware of its hazards.

Early in canto 26, the poet beats a hasty retreat from such crowing. When he thinks now of Ulysses and the flaming tongues, his words, again in present tense, could be read as a reconsideration of his boasting in the lines quoted above:

> I grieved then and now I grieve again
> as my thoughts turn to what I saw,
> and more than is my way, I curb my powers

> lest they run on where virtue fails to guide them,
> so that, if friendly star or something better still
> has granted me its boon, I don't refuse the gift. (26:19–24)

This passage shows how seriously the poet takes the question of literary fame. Otherwise he wouldn't need to recant an insignificant mistake.

Among other possibilities, the ditch in canto 26 suggests the kind of pitfall that threatens great verbal accomplishments: the tendency to focus those accomplishments on oneself (think of Latini's "follow your star" in canto 15) rather than on "something better still." To a Christian writer, this would be the literary artist's version of the ultimate sin of pride. Though you can feel the exceptional pull of what this ditch represents on both pilgrim and poet, neither has quite fallen in. Otherwise it's a different poem. In any case, one thing seems sure. Dante the poet has language power on his mind in canto 26.

You could reinforce this claim by asking students what poet, pilgrim, guide, the Ulysses in Dante, and his Homeric prototype have in common. Obviously they are all language masters with a proven record of influencing people around them by the mere power of their words. Since the exercise of that power in their respective narratives leads to greatly varied results, it is fair to claim that this canto is gauging the uses to which verbal gifts should be put. What uses of verbal virtuosity would a Christian defend, and where do its uses become damnable? Maybe the poet's ultimate question about language is this: what are words, especially literary words, for? Without some answer to that question, you can't evaluate specific cases of language use except pragmatically, according to whether they accomplish whatever ends the user has selected. It is hard to see how a Christian like Dante would be comfortable with pragmatic logic, especially for some of the weightiest instances of verbal construction.

Reading the entire *Commedia* with these questions in mind will show you how large they loom to its author. From one angle or another, he brings them up repeatedly. Some version of this issue probably poses itself eventually to most great writers, Christian or not. But you certainly don't want to neglect the force of Christian belief here. Urge your students to frame as sharp a working hypothesis as the text will allow distinguishing right speech from its opposite. How exactly does the poet's Christianity figure in any such generalization?

Leaving aside the Homeric Odysseus, whom Dante must have known only as a type, you can array the remaining four language virtuosos above on a continuum from praiseworthy to contemptible. In *Inferno*, Ulysses's tongue energizes a "mad flight" that results in his own death and that of his men. That ought to place him pretty far out toward the negative pole. In its context, Ulysses's fifty-two-line speech at the end of *Inferno* 26 plays out a cautionary tale for poet and pilgrim, representing a road not to take, with the pilgrim's early love poetry steering in Ulysses's direction and Virgil's *Aeneid* pointing away. So the poet is resting a lot of weight on that speech. It is one of the *Commedia*'s great moments. Notice that once Virgil opens the gates by urging Ulysses to speak, out comes monologue in a flood of words showing little regard for audience or occasion. Observe how little interest Ulysses has in conversation with his visitors. Virgil and Dante could be anyone. His real audience is himself. You will already begin to suspect that, true to *Inferno* form, this speaker's words and manner will incriminate him unintendedly. If the foregoing claims are persuasive, the incrimination will arise from the misuse of persuasive language.

Ultimately you come down to the familiar crux: what's wrong with the picture of this character? What sets this canto apart is how much cultural, religious/philosophical, and historical weight it can bring to bear on this question. Though Ulysses's speech is blatantly called in question by its disastrous ending, a Christian evaluation would want to look at more than results. Where are the elements of Ulysses's speech and the other details comprising his portrait that become more incriminating the more you think about them, regardless of where they lead? Rather than trying to respond a little to this big question here, I want to propose avenues of possible investigation in the exercises below. Since my previous categories would overlap so much in this case, I'll try to create a more sequential arrangement below.

Exercises

1. Contrapasso: how is God's management of those situated in the eighth bolgia fitting? A good answer to this question probably requires two steps. First identify exactly what form of fraud is being punished here. Though Virgil enumerates the sins that Ulysses and Diomedes mourn "in their flame" (26:58–63), given Ulysses's speech, it is hard to see Virgil's list as getting fully to the point. I'm claiming that, as always, some perversion of soul is being illuminated here, one involving the corruption of some human potential.

    In trying to identify that faculty or potential, you have the unique advantage of having a second canto to look at dealing with the same shortcoming. In canto 27 the flame of Guido da Montefeltro speaks to pilgrim and guide at length from the same ditch. This gives the Ulysses portrait a bit of context. So what do Guido da Montefeltro and Ulysses have in common, in both past deeds and quality of being? Obviously both were in a position to exercise their language gifts to great effect, and though some of what they say may seem defensible, their own verbal powers have contributed to their fall. So you'll need to look at least in part to character, to some unbalanced inclination in both of them, something involving a fraudulent relation to others that gives shape to the flaming tongue the way the body gives shape and life to the clothing that covers it.

From there, you'll then need to analyze the imagery, mainly in canto 26, that delineates the general punishment the figures here are suffering or have made for themselves:

> . . . each flame conceals a sinner. (26:42).

> These spirits stand within the flames.
> Each one is wrapped in that in which he burns. (26:47–48)

> [Minos] said: "Here comes a sinner for the thieving fire."
> And so, just as you see me [Guido speaking], I am damned,
> cloaked as I am. And as I go, I grieve. (27:127–29)

And a few other details to the same effect. Basically, then, these souls are now little more than tongues, moving around the gullet of this ditch, stolen and burned by the flame that clothes them. How is that fitting? How does someone's tongue become not just expressive or ornamental, but consuming? And in what mode are these images apt: as an ingenious piece of ironic retribution or as the image of what people like Ulysses and Guido have made of their souls before they die?

2.   To promote some closer reading under the same question, have your students consider how Dante uses the language of dress at key points in the passages cited in my first question. The souls of those in this bolgia are "wrapped" and "cloaked" in their respective tongues of flame. Through these two participles, Dante encourages you to consider how perverted verbal giftedness in relation to its user is like clothing on a body (body: clothing = eighth-bolgia soul: tongue of flame). What does that analogy add to your understanding of the characters here? How can the cloak of language virtuousity steal the soul it adorns? What would be the difference between this kind of language adornment and better garb?

3.   Now consider the intricacies of the portrait Dante paints of Ulysses individually. If Ulysses is like previous infernal speakers who tell their stories, his narrative will reveal a lot about what got him here. If not, how would Dante justify the length of his monologue? I think you will find plenty in that speech that will incriminate Ulysses and attach his fraudulent behavior

to the abuse of a particular human faculty. How far and in what ways does this famous speech (26:90–142) undermine its speaker?

For a start, you might note Ulysses's description of what moved him to make the journey. Taken by itself "fervor . . . to gain experience of the world/and learn about man's vices, and his worth" is hard to fault. Such inquisitive ardor has benefited our species in many ways. But you'll notice that Ulysses doesn't posit this emotion in isolation. He sets it against "tenderness for a son," "filial duty toward my aged father," and "the love I owed Penelope that would have made her glad." Here's another case where Dante confronts your students with a genuine conflict of values, one that it wouldn't do to oversimplify. Remind them that their first job here is to interpret the text, to come up with arguments for how the poet wants readers to weigh one set of values against another. Dante wouldn't be doing Ulysses justice if this problem could be easily resolved.

Again, you look for context. One obvious piece is Ulysses's present position deep in hell. And you'd have to put weight on the deaths of Ulysses and his men at the end of what Ulysses now admits was a "mad flight." In addition to these explicit references to the text, some com- mentators find here an allusion to the contrasting motives and values of Aeneas in Virgil's epic. According to the Hollanders, while Ulysses "denies his family feeling for Telemachus, Laertes, and Penelope in order to make his voyage," Aeneas is "loyal to Ascanius, Anchises, and Creusa" and "as Virgil hardly tires of calling him, pius, a 'family man' if ever there was one" (*Inferno* 26:94–99n). One of the most memorable images from the *Aeneid* is of Aeneas the Trojan leaving the havoc of burning Troy, holding his son by the hand, carrying his aged father on his shoulders, and leading out his wife (at least at first). What image would Dante's Ulysses want to set beside that one?

You'll also notice that in whipping up his men's enthusiasm for the trip, Ulysses appeals to their pride as Greeks, against the other option of being "beasts or brutes." To intensify the heat of this appeal, he employs the demagogue's stock-in-trade: culturally manipulative abstractions carrying either/or implications. He goads them tauntingly: in effect, "You old guys are still Greeks aren't you? Have you no curiosity left? Are you not still interested in pursuing virtue and knowledge?" A pretty effective set of chal- lenges to manly ethnic pride, wouldn't you say? As with Francesca, it won't do to treat this character simplistically. Dante's Ulysses is still the master rhetorician. So where would you find fault in his list of appeals? How would Dante want readers to evaluate this character without undervaluing the virtues he cites and embodies? What accounts for his position in hell?

4.   For those who know classical epic, Dante's poem has a lot to gain from the comparison of conceptions of heroism. Ulysses, Aeneas, and Dante are heroes of epic narratives with comedic endings. Hence highly comparable. Through the differences between Aeneas and Ulysses, Dante can sharpen your understanding of what qualities define the hero of a Christian epic.

Then consider epic devices Dante may allude to in canto 26, as at the beginning of *Inferno*. There he wanted to evoke comparison with classical epic, the better to indicate his poem's aspiration to the status and form of a Christian epic. Here he brings up epic to set his character against the background of classical heroism. It is a contrast, maybe in some ways a development, of values.

Like classical epics, Ulysses's narrative begins *in medias res*, in the middle of things. In the *Iliad* and *Odyssey*, Homer uses that device to provide unity of focus for his poems. Out of a wealth of possible Trojan War materials, the *Iliad* will interest itself in a few days toward the end of the war when a quarrel between two of the greatest Greek leaders provides a way to examine the glories and shortcomings of the early Greek heroic ideal. Unlike other extant Trojan War homecoming stories, the *Odyssey* opens when the great hero is at probably the lowest point in his life, having been for seven years marooned powerless, possessionless, and stripped of heroic identity on an island controlled by the nymph Calypso. The *Odyssey* is the story not just of a successful return home but of how one particularly resourceful hero manages to make his way back from nowhere to his former kingly station. Where Homer breaks into these stories tells you what they are about. You could make a similar case for the beginning of Virgil's *Aeneid*.

What's the difference for Dante's Ulysses, who observing the same convention, launches into his story in the middle where "I took leave of Circe." The determinants of this opening seem to have less to do with the integrity of the story to follow than with the psychology of the narrator. Once that tongue starts to quiver, it can neither be stopped nor made to show any sensitivity to situation or audience. It just runs on, machine-like. This is the monologue of a great rhetorician gone obsessive. If so, then what psychological malformation explains this loss of savvy? How does your answer here deepen your understanding of what has situated Ulysses in this damned gullet?

Ulysses's speech also includes a smaller-scale epic motif, or *topos*, but one that will be very familiar to readers of Homer and Virgil. Call it the determined-attempt topos. When someone in classical epic is urgently attempting to accomplish some difficult task, he valiantly tries, and usually fails, three times. Almost always three times. In the underworld, Odysseus tries three times to embrace his mother's shade. In the courtyard of Odysseus's palace in Ithaka, his son Telemachus tries three times to string the mighty bow. In trying to approach the Mount of Purgatory, Ulysses involves himself and his men in an ill-fated venture that Dante has him similarly couch under the rule of three. The epic context adds weight to Ulysses's use of the device here, perhaps suggesting the seriousness and difficulty of what he is attempting and the probability of ultimate failure. Your students could make a good project out of finding examples of this form in Homer or Virgil to use for examining how Dante is using it here, but a bit of class discussion could do the job too.

5. Finally, some consideration is due the two Dantes in canto 26. For its duration, there is not much distance between them. Both feel strongly the attraction of the power housed in this ditch and both grieve in witnessing its condition in hell. It is as if the poet briefly forgets himself here, so that rather than the pilgrim maturing toward becoming the poet, here the poet slides back toward the Dante he used to be. What is the point of this brief reversal? In addition to whatever else your students might come up with, you might point out that this canto humanizes the poet a little. Apparently, having angels in purgatory wipe the symbols of the seven deadly sins from your forehead and being given a vision of the divine light in paradise are not sufficient to illuminate permanently the mind of a successful pilgrim. The poet still has to struggle at times with old demons. Why would the author of the poem, as opposed to poet and pilgrim, want it this way?

Close Reading

1. Prominent Word Repetitions: Two Cases. Take a look at the two uses of "virtue" in this canto, one by Dante the poet in present tense in line 22, the other by Ulysses in line 120. Virtue is one of those potentially dangerous abstractions that can be used manipulatively because they are so readily sentimentalized. How many people around you have really thought through what the virtues are? I can guarantee you that Dante has, with the term's use in this canto as one indication of the result. So what is the meaning of this term in the mouths of these two speakers? Please take meaning here to include both content and use. How does their use of this word help to distinguish Greek hero from Christian poet?

    Similarly for the word *cammino*, meaning journey, which appears here in Ulysses's speech at line 122 and in the poet's in the poem's famous first line. This is as comprehensive a word as this poem has to offer. The entire poem and Ulysses's poem-within-a-poem are governed by its structure. Much has been said above about different kinds of journeys, so let's just point out here that you might use this term as a good way to initiate the comparison. What are the differences implicit in the two uses of this term?

2. Two similes: it's not too common in *Inferno* to find the poet placing two similes with the same tenor back-to-back, but he does so in canto 26 in lines 25 to 42. He constructs two elaborate nine-line similes right after declaring that he will "curb my powers/lest they run on where virtue fail to guide them." He uses both similes to describe the sight from a distance of the flame-souls who inhabit this bolgia, the first one dealing with their number, the second with their movement. Why this figurative flourish right at the point where the poet expresses misgivings about artistic excess? Misgivings and similes certainly seem to be somehow connected. I don't have a good answer to this question, but I can point out one unusual feature of the similes. The figure doing the seeing, the one who represents the pilgrim looking down on the flames, disappears in the tenor of both similes. So the presence of the peasant in the first simile should lead to something like "so I saw that many flames" in line 31. But the Italian includes no "I." The peasant has no stated analogue in the rest of the simile. The pilgrim has been elided. So also for Elisha, "the one who was avenged by bears" in the second simile. Where there should be a "so I saw" at line 40, again the "I" has been eliminated. I find this apparent anomaly at least interesting and maybe pertinent to the question of how this misgivings/similes package is functioning here. I might be stretching a little, but can we see this effacement of the "I" in these two prominent figures of speech in the context of the artist's avowed intention to curb the artistic egotism he flaunted in the previous canto?

Projects

This canto can generate projects galore. One kind might deal with adaptations of the Ulysses figure in literature or film. You could have students compare the representation of this figure and then look for reasons for the differences. Roman appropriations of this character were generally negative in tone, which probably tells you more about Roman attitudes toward Greek culture than about Ulysses.

Another kind could focus on the idea of the hero. Joseph Campbell's writings have popularized the notion of a hero's journey archetype. Though I'm skeptical about one-paradigm-fits-all schemas like his, Campbell's work has done a lot to get a wide range of people thinking about what a hero is. One thing you'll notice if you look at the history of the term is its expanding range of reference.

In Homer it refers to a small class of aristocratic fighters who "fight in the front" of the battle lines in pursuing their own honor. Gradually "hero" expands to include characters in other kinds of literature and ultimately to refer to any great person who behaves nobly under fire. Nowadays the protagonist of any piece of literature can be called a hero, as can real people with no class status at all who do great things in extreme circumstances. This pattern of extension of a word's lexical reach by expansion of frame of reference is common. You seldom see the reverse: narrowing of coverage over time. Investigating the development of this particular term would be a good way to lead your students to some conclusions about how language works.

Then you can look at the term's meaning. That, by definition, is culturally and temporally relative. What do people mean by "hero" in other places and/or times? Who would qualify as contemporary American cultural heroes? Would your students agree with some critics that nowadays the term is used so loosely and frequently that its meaning has been sadly diluted? To answer that question, your students could again look for an essence to the idea of a hero across place and time and then determine whether that essence is preserved in the way the term is typically used today. I'm betting you will be able to think of many good classroom projects stemming from reflection and research on this pregnant term. I sometimes had good luck with my students doing that.

Bridging the Gaps

I want to reaffirm here my claim that the *Inferno* is an ideal work to get your students talking about issues that divide them. In my experience, these are generally based on inherited dispositions. You hear their parents' voices in theirs. Whatever the merit of the positions your high-school students take, rarely have they thought them through for themselves much. One of your jobs as a literature teacher is to set up situations that prompt them to. Toward that end, innocent-seeming terms like "hero" can be particularly useful. "Hero" has a core meaning that is universal enough to establish common ground: every society has its heroes. But from its core idea, the term spins off variations across cultures and times. Questions about what a hero is and has been, here and there, can provide your students the occasion to talk candidly about cultural, ethnic, and religious differences. No matter what your own beliefs, you should be trying to produce more reflective, knowledgeable Christians, Muslims, Jews, Buddhists, agnostics, or atheists. We literature teachers should be looking to instill knowledge, not so much for empowerment (on the AP test and beyond) as for understanding. Dante can help with this, particularly in canto 26.

9

Schism

CANTO 28

These days, a book like this one has to include a chapter on canto 28 because Dante places Mohammed here. He is among those who, according to the Hollanders (2002), "either cause schism in others or themselves lead schismatic groups" (26:35n). Etymologically, "schism" comes from a Greek word meaning "split." All the schismatics in this canto played an essential role in one or more instances of splitting what Dante thinks should be kept whole. Since they are in one of the circles of the fraudulent, they must have used the cunning of their minds maliciously to effect these destructive divisions. Dante regards Mohammed as a Christian schismatic, founding "what Dante considered a rival sect rather than a new religion, Islam" (26:22–31n.). As this quote suggests, Dante knew little about Mohammed, and what information he had was generally mistaken. In trying to make sense of Dante's depiction of Mohammed and the religion he founded, your students should keep firmly in mind how flawed the assumptions were on which this depiction is based.

You may notice again what form divine justice takes here: a devil with a sword splits all the splitters in a manner commensurate with their specific schismatic act(s). Thus Mohammed, who (according to Dante) divided Christianity, in effect cleaving the body of Christ, is "cleft from the chin down to where men fart" (26:24), with his innards hanging out in as disgusting a set of images as Dante takes the time to develop in *Inferno*. Dante seems to regard Ali's role in the division of Islam into two separate sects, Sunni and Shia, as less blameworthy than Mohammed's, because Ali's wounding is less extensive. If so, you might do well to question what the difference is. At the very least, Ali's facial wounding "from chin to forelock" would seem to accord Islam some respect since one can be positioned here for dividing it.

Is the contrapasso here retributive or representational? The latter, I remind you, finds so close a relation between sin and punishment that the soul's situation in hell can be seen as an external representation of its state at the time of death. It is admittedly a little harder to make my usual case for the latter here, but I'll give it a try. I'd start by pointing out that for all the complexity of the views implied in this poem, Dante is conservative when it comes to inherited forms of order. He would by temperament favor the preservation of traditional familial, political, and religious structures. When he innovates, it is not to undermine a given tradition but to draw out some of its undeveloped implications. Axiomatic with him is probably something like the platonic idea that the good is fostered when each of the parts of a system fulfills its role effectively. In the *Republic*, Plato defines justice in the state as the result of each class performing its designated function. He then draws a famous analogy between the structure of the state and that of individual souls in it. A just human soul is one in which the energizing appetites and emotions submit to the control of the faculty of reason. So justice in a person or a state is a picture of component parts in unified balance. (I find that you don't have to approve of the political implications of this idea to be interested in its psychological ones.) Regarding individual humans at least, Dante seems to subscribe to something like this picture of a well-ordered soul.

So I have to argue that the split in the bodies of schismatics in Canto 28 reflects a division in their souls, a kind of internal discord that would have led them to commit such divisive acts in the life above. Before he divided others, Mohammed first had to divide himself. That inference is supported by his first words in the canto at lines 30 and 31: "See how I rend myself,/see how mangled is Mohammed!" This exclamation connects passive with active, being mangled with mangling oneself, punishment by God with self-punishment. That's just what the idea of representational divine justice might require. I'm claiming that to Dante, some form of self-rending explains Mohammed's schismatic founding of Islam: his appetite for power, or position, or perhaps his hatred for the church, got the best of the better angels of his nature.

What would the opposite of such a divided soul look like? Appropriately enough, canto 28 does provide a possible answer to that question in lines that interrupt the narrative to express the poet's present-tense understanding:

> But I stayed on to watch the troop
> and saw a thing I would be loath
> to mention without further proof,
>
> were I not comforted by conscience,
> the bosom friend that fortifies a man
> beneath the armor of an honest heart. (112–17)

The quasi-proverbial language in the second tercet expresses how the poet would structure interior well-being. Fundamental to that is a well-functioning moral faculty that is protected from corruption by an honest heart. Divided souls must therefore be riven by dishonesty within themselves, weakening the defenses of conscience so that it becomes vulnerable to other interior forces. In *Inferno* these forces produce incontinence, violence, and fraud. Purgatory divides up this territory more concisely, probably in order of decreasing seriousness, into seven deadly sins: pride, envy, wrath, sloth, covetousness, gluttony, and lust. However you cut it, the combination of an active conscience and an honest heart would show the way to avoid damaging egotistic behavior and provide the strength to follow that way. In a psyche dominated by these two protectors, emotional energies and appetites could not but assume subordinate positions. There you would have it: a balanced soul. When that hierarchy isn't in place, base forms of desire can take over, creating a self at odds with itself. Such a condition will have to reflect itself in external behavior. Only a thus-mangled Mohammed could have divided up the religious sphere as he did. Since he never repented this action, his condition in hell is then a reflection of his inner condition at death. This I take to be Dante's position. (Or so I claim, straining a little.)

In the last thirty lines of the canto (112f), the pilgrim encounters the shade of Bertran de Born, probably the poem's most memorable image of the operation of the contrapasso. In fact, it is only here at the end of Bertran's speech (28:142) that Dante makes use of this term, a standard in *Inferno* commentaries. A twelfth-century Provencal troubadour poet, Bertran is situated here because of his counsel to Prince Henry, which launched this "Young King" into rebellion against his father, Henry II of England. Thus Bertran was an essential cause of familial division at a level affecting everyone in England. He helped separate the head of family and country from its other parts. His disturbing condition here, head speaking from hand, seems obviously fitting retributively. This advisor, who separated the king from his son and from those of his subjects who joined the son's rebellion, must carry his own severed head.

To defend a reading of Bertran's image here as more than retributive, let me call in support from Mark Musa (1996) in his edition of *Inferno*:

> The figure of Bertran de Born suddenly takes center stage, thrusting forward from the crowd. The grotesque image of the headless trunk presented in the first tercet [lines 118–20] is intensified in the second tercet [lines 121–23] by the head's "disembodied" speech ("Oh me!"). His stance, holding his head like a lantern, is a macabre commentary on his sin. The head should have been the illuminator and guide of the

body's actions, but in Bertran de Born's case, the head's reason gave way to the body's greed and irreverence. Bertran de Born's punishment is especially appropriate because his sin was an act of political decapitation, amounting to an attempt to undermine rightful heads of state. (18:118–23n)

Musa's commentary on this canto offers more to the same effect. To have acted as he did, Bertran must have disconnected his head from his body in order to serve the latter's impulses. His image in hell dreadfully reflects that disconnection. That's something beyond mere retribution.

Exercises

1. Other than all the usual issues that you might explore in questions on this canto (pilgrim versus poet, the nature of the contrapasso, Virgil's virtues and limitations as guide, etc.), you might use this canto as an excuse to focus on one of the most pressing subjects for contemporary Western audiences: the nature of Islam in precept and practice. Dante's assessment of Mohammed is hard to take seriously because it is based on faulty knowledge of him and the religion he founded. Even though no one nowadays need share that kind of ignorance, many do. As usual, such misunderstanding hamstrings current attempts to respond effectively and appropriately to events in the Muslim world. As a primary text remedy, you might use this occasion to select some essential Koranic verses for your students to study. The web abounds in sites dedicated to helping you do this. They come flavored by various intentions. For your purposes here, make sure to choose a site that is sympathetic, or at least objectively fair-minded, toward the Muslim faith. Though my knowledge in this area is as superficial as can be, I might also recommend *The Essential Koran* by Thomas Cleary (1994). He's a renowned translator of religious texts. In this short book, he collects, organizes, and translates various passages that he considers representative of the fundamentals of Islam. You would learn a lot about the faith there while gaining a feel for the beauty of Koranic verse. Somehow you need to learn enough to help your students start building, at least in their minds, that most essential of contemporary bridges, the one connecting the Western world to the Middle East. Shouldn't you regard that almost as a literature teacher's duty nowadays?

2. Tthe problem of fraud. Though it's not difficult to apply the charge of fraud to someone like Bertran de Born, Mohammed is a harder case. Even

allowing Dante's misunderstanding of him and his religion, how can the Prophet's actions be considered fraudulent? You would be looking for an answer that keeps this section of *Inferno* internally consistent. I have trouble finding one.

3. The contrapasso of Bertran de Born. His severed head in hand constitutes one of the most memorable images in *Inferno*. How is it appropriate to what we can know about Bertran? Some reading in Bertran's poetry, a good bit of which still exists, would help here. The Hollanders call him "one of the great poets of war of his or any other time" (28:130–38n). The matured author of the *Commedia* might not see eye to eye with Bertran on questions of poetic content or style. But your students won't necessarily need that background to make some sense of the imagery of Bertran's contrapasso. They can just focus on his decisive misdeed: encouraging Prince Henry to rebel against his father, King Henry II, leading to the prince's death.

To develop the image further, Dante compares the carried head to a lantern:

> And by his hair he held his severed head
> swinging in his hand as if it were a lantern. (28:121–22)

Musa's interpretation of this passage (quoted above) justifies both a retributive, eye-for-an-eye reading (as he decapitated, so he is decapitated) and a representational one (he subordinated head to body, which is what we see imaged here where the head acts as no more than a means to light the body's path). Bertran's poetry might add testimony to such body-over-mind inversion.

To complicate matters further, the poet works in a little theological context:

> Of himself he made himself a lamp,
> and they were two in one and one in two.
> How this can be He knows who so ordains it (28:124–26)

Here I think your students, maybe especially the Catholics among them, will hear a reference to the theological relation between God the Father and His Son. They might also remember biblical correspondences likening Jesus to a head and his church to its body.

However your students understand these devices, they will probably agree that the Bertran imagery constitutes a fitting culmination to the canto. Christian thought employs images of organic unity to describe relations between parts: of God's nature and of the man-God relationship. That kind of background adds negative gravity to the dismemberment of Bertran's body, if any were needed. So given what we know about Bertran, what is the significance of that severed head? Merely retributively appropriate?

10

Ice

CANTOS 31–33

An icy surprise? I certainly got one the first time I got to cantos 31 and 32. Dante has to be counting on his reversal of fire-and-brimstone expectations for a lot of the effect of the last few cantos. Since it's Dante, you might have expected something inventive, but who envisioned Satanic ice? And yet I want to claim that had you and I been better readers, ice is exactly what we should have predicted. After all, Dante's God has structured the cosmos with earth at the greatest possible distance from himself. In the outer heavenly circle called the empyrean, he is sunlike in his spacious, warm luminosity. Logically, then, the center of earth should be confining, cold, and dark, with the frozen lake of Cocytus as the pit of hell, its ninth and smallest circle. This principle of inversion, whereby the bottom of hell is the negative reflection of the lofty reaches of heaven, structures much of Dante's thinking in the last few cantos of *Inferno*.

Before the pilgrim reaches the actual ice, he has to confront the ninth circle's guards. These mythological giants are reminiscent of the other emblematic figures sprinkled throughout *Inferno*, but especially of the forbidding Furies and Medusa who guard the towered fortress of Dis in canto 9. Nimrod, Ephialtes, Briareus, Tityus, Typhon, and Antaeus are stationed right next to the bank separating the eighth circle from the ninth. They loom up before Dante and Virgil like "a range of lofty towers" in a fortified city. Their lower bodies are hidden by the bank so that only their upper halves are visible to guide and pilgrim. Aside from Antaeus, all these titanic sentinels share a history of rebellion against the gods or God himself. What might these emblematic figures represent?

As before, it's difficult to extract this essence here with anything like absolute conviction, but not hard to list some elements that good attempts will have to account for:

- the precedents: previous emblems representing some form of sick or unbalanced human soul or the perversion of some human faculty
- the giants' murky milieu
- their relation to Satan, whose name in Hebrew means "to oppose"
- their size, immobility, and depth in hell
- Nimrod's gibberish and the lack of intelligible speech from any of his fellows
- Ephialtes's anger when Virgil describes Briareus as more fearsome than he
- Virgil's flattery of Antaeus with praise of his hunting exploits and a promise that the pilgrim will make him famous back in the world above (guide and pilgrim need this giant's help in getting down onto the ice)

So what is that quality that is deep in the human soul, huge and powerful; difficult to see, to access with language, and to understand; related to Satan, hence oppositional; hyperconcerned with fame and with being accounted better than any competitors? Into what essence can these features be distilled?

Pride, say the Hollanders (31:28–33n), has been the traditional answer to these questions. They trace this response all the way back to the influential fourteenth-century *Inferno* commentary of Pietro Alighieri, Dante's son, with many subsequent commentators agreeing since. You'd have to say it stands on pretty solid ground. After all, overweening pride is what is held to have motivated Satan's rebellion against God. Here's C. S. Lewis (2009) on pride:

> According to Christian teachers, the essential vice, the utmost evil, is Pride. Unchastity, anger, greed, drunkenness, and all that, are mere flea bites in comparison: it was through Pride that the devil became the devil: Pride leads to every other vice: it is the complete anti-God state of mind. (book 3, chapter 8)

If pride underlies all other sins, the idea of emblems of pride on the ground floor of hell makes good structural sense. Likewise for the emotional appropriateness of the giants' attitudes. It's not hard to see pride behind Antaeus's desire for fame and praise and under Ephialtes's angry inability to tolerate anything less than top position.

To season the rest of the ingredients listed above, let me stir in a little W. H. Auden (1952):

I could watch a man all his life, and I should never know for certain whether or not he was proud, for the actions which we call proud may have quite other causes. Pride is rightly called the root of all sin, because it is invisible to the one who is guilty of it and he can only infer it from results. These facts of existence are expressed in the Christian doctrines of Man's creation and his fall. . . . Man fell through pride, a wish to become God, to derive his existence from himself. (8)

Pride is thus hard to see and understand, powerful in its effects, situated deep beneath the light of everyday consciousness, and fundamentally perverted in its understanding of its relation to the divine. Allegorically, pride vies for control of that part of the soul that deals with the self in its relation to others and to its creator. As Satan shows, give pride the chance and it will disastrously mishandle these relationships by making the individual self paramount. To Christians, doesn't putting self in place of God constitute rebellion in its most fundamental form? All other forms of opposition start there. All these implications resonate with Dante's gigantic imagery in canto 31. One of Dante's key insights, expressed in the funnel shape of hell and all Inferno's contrapassos, is that sin may at first seem liberating but is ultimately confining. More so as sins worsen. Pride, as the root of all sin would then entail ultimate confinement. Hence its association with the giants' immobility followed by images of beings stuck in the ice in hell's circle of least circumference.

With Lewis, Auden, and the Hollanders in my corner, then, I want to maintain that in the last four cantos of *Inferno*, Dante is working out the problem of how to represent pride appropriately. You'll see that he dovetails it nicely with his master strategy for the construction of the pit of hell. Logically enough, these cantos will feature imagery and situations in diametrical opposition to those of the blessedly virtuous in heaven.

If you find the above arguments convincing, you might entertain my contention that canto 33 acts as the emotional climax of *Inferno*, tipping Satan's canto 34 into anticlimax. It centers on one Count Ugolino, who conspired with Archbishop Ruggieri to seize power in Pisa in 1288. As partners in political intrigue, the two were guilty of betraying party and country at several points during their history together. In one of the poem's most memorable accounts, Ugolino describes the archbishop's ultimate betrayal and imprisonment of him together with his four young sons in Pisa's "Tower of Hunger." To maximize this narrative's impact, Dante uses a little poetic license: historical sources show that by early 1289, two sons and two grandsons starved to death in the tower with Ugolino. I doubt this alteration will bother your students much. They will probably find Ugolino's imprisonment story one of the most moving, and disturbing, in the poem. I certainly do.

At the end of canto 32 (124f), pilgrim and guide come upon the souls of these two former coconspirators "frozen in a single hole" in the ice. They find Ugolino biting into the nape of Ruggieri's neck, and then at the beginning of canto 33 pausing to wipe his bloody mouth on the hair of his victim. Right away the suggestion is that canto 33 might have something to do with the consumption of human flesh. Figuratively, you might construe the pair's betrayals of party and city as acts of predation. You know you've got hold of a rather grisly motif when you get to Ugolino's description of starvation in the tower during which he first gnaws his own hand and then, maybe, the bodies of his sons. His "Then fasting had more power than grief" is another one of *Inferno*'s memorably damning single-line admissions. It's similar to Francesca's suggestive "That day we read in it no further" but more horrifyingly ambiguous. Did Ugolino eat his sons? Though critics are divided on this question, I want to argue that Dante leaves the answer unclear because it doesn't much matter.

If Dante intends to depict deep hell as the converse of paradise, then what is the heavenly counterpart of the eating of flesh? If you ask the question in that way, some of your students might easily perceive the obvious response. I needed help from a John Freccero (1986) essay to do so (152–66). We know that civilized Romans in the century after Christ's death looked down on Christians as barbaric because their rituals seemed to celebrate the eating of human flesh. Romans thought Christian communicants were cannibalistic. Though it isn't hard to see how ill-informed outsiders could make that mistake, we can laugh at the irony in it today. It runs ridiculously deep. But in that ironic distance between cannibalism and holy sacrament lies much of what Dante wants to communicate in canto 33.

In mode of development, Ugolino clearly stands in the line of Francesca and Ulysses. That's pretty fast company. All three are striking presentations of what I called literary persons in a previous chapter. Ask your students what these three portraits have in common. They might identify such similarities as the following. They all deliver masterful performances in the art of unconscious first person self-incrimination. What separates them from some of the other characters in *Inferno* is narrative: the poet has all of them undercut themselves by beginning their stories in medias res, at their moral/spiritual crux. All three of the stories lead, for example, to destruction not just of the speaker but of one or more others close at hand. All three characters practice the art of self-exculpation pretty deftly in front of pilgrim and guide. None of the three is repentant, which reveals itself in tone as much as any other way. By that I mean that you feel inappropriateness in the attitude of the tellers to their materials. Francesca still seems to delight in the eroticism of her destructive liaison with Paolo. Ulysses likewise brims with pride at the verbal strategies he deployed to convince his crew to row rashly into purgatorial waters. For Ugolino's monologue, the tonal case is a little harder to pin down, but don't you feel something wrong not just in the events he relates but in the telling? However you get at Ugolino's shortcomings, it should be clear that he doesn't fully understand his situation in hell. Maybe that's what Dante means by having lost the good of intellect (*Inferno* 3:18).

The resulting portraits, then, are rich in dramatic irony. At least I hope you think so. As reading the critics will show, not all commentators make the sharp a distinction between how these characters take themselves and how the poet wants readers to take them. To me, failure to perceive this kind of irony has to lead to a misreading of the poem.

Of course, the point of mentioning these other characters here must be to shed light on Dante's treatment of Ugolino. The ironies in Ugolino's narrative might be best approached through the oppositions Dante sets up it. Notice how often Ugolino appeals for sympathy once he starts to speak. The Hollanders point to numerous references to weeping and grief in Ugolino's speech, with several more mentions of weeping later in the canto. In a speech so insistently about tears, ask your students what Dante sets up as their contrary? They will soon come upon line 49: "I was so turned to stone inside I did not weep." Here stone stands in strong contrast to that quality in humans that leads us to weep for others. (Your students may notice that while Ugolino talks a lot about weeping in this canto, we never actually see him cry.) You can see how ice fits this picture too, as a hardening of something that would normally flow. The causality seems to run this way: because Ugolino had already made for himself a heart of stone or ice, he was not able to respond to his own sons with fatherly humanity after the door to that tower was nailed shut. Now, not even remembering can bring him to tears. Whatever else all this suggests, you'd have to conclude that this canto centers on human emotion in its foundational position in the human soul.

Several commentators, including the Hollanders, cite a biblical line as implicit in Ugolino's narrative, specifically in regard to the sons' request for bread (33:39). It is from the Gospel of Luke: "If a son shall ask bread of any of you that is a father, will he give him a stone?" (King James Version Luke 11:11). Jesus is commenting on a parable he has just related. The Hollanders' note on this allusion is particularly helpful (33:49n). One implication is that bread figures in Ugolino's story as another contrary to stone. So pattern-wise the poet stands bread and tears on one side against stone and ice on the other. Juxtaposed with the image of their weeping, the sons' mention of bread to the father suggests their need for sustenance is not just physical. All he can offer them is stone. Dante is pointing to a stony heart as the contrary of what Mark Twain called "the good heart," that fundamentally sympathetic human faculty, warm and fluid, that sustains itself and those nearby. Compassion, sympathy, commiseration—it's no accident that the English language, and probably most others, includes several words that denote "feeling with" someone else. To Dante, apparently, the life without such fellow-feeling is essentially incomplete. Petrification of the soul's liquid heart leaves you with something less than a human being. Something whose sign might well be called bestial.

There is also the question of reference to Christian communion in this canto. Here, as I said, I'm following John Freccero (1986, 152–66), who emphasizes the significance of the sons' offer to their father at 33:61–63:

> Father, we would suffer less
> if you would feed on us: you clothed us
> in this wretched flesh—now strip it off.

Freccero hears this as an echo of Christ's sacrificial offer to mankind, given concrete form in Jesus's language during his last supper with his disciples: "And he took bread, gave thanks and broke it, and gave it to them, saying, 'This is my body given for you; do this in remembrance of me'" (New International Version Luke 22:19). Dante reinforces the Jesus connection in Gaddo's dying plea: "O father, why won't you help me?" (33:69). You can hear in this line an allusion to Jesus's similar question from the cross.

Freccero claims that readers should see reflected in the sons' offer something like a Eucharistic gesture. According to Freccero, Ugolino fails to hear in their words "a redemptive possibility" echoing "the Eucharistic sacrifice." He sees Ugolino's failure as "an inability to interpret the Christian hope contained in the words of his children." A better interpretation could have allowed his sons "a shared grief and a reconciliation to their father." He might have helped them wrest some communal solace out of their terrible fate, perhaps by finding a way to give meaning to their suffering. Dante alludes to the Eucharist to underscore how damnable is Ugolino's failure to ease in any way his sons' passage out of this world. Something like this is Freccero's thesis. I find it illuminating.

The antithesis to the stony interior that Ugolino brought to the Tower of Hunger would then be the spirit in which earnest communicants approach the Eucharist. What spirit is that? Something grounded more deeply in the heart than in the head, according to this canto, but certainly not a heart full of pride. Beyond that observation, as someone outside the faith, I have trouble going. But I imagine some of your students will have a lot to say in distinguishing the spirit of Ugolino with his sons from that of a devout Christian approaching the Communion rail.

This canto appropriately rests on a bedrock question: what grounds the connection between one human being and another: the ability to enter sympathetically into another's life, especially at times of acute suffering? Tears would then represent to Dante the *sine qua non* of humanity, without which there is no sympathy, no love, no real human communion of any kind. The life with that emotional reservoir iced up, Dante suggests, is not a human life. The pilgrim's last sight of Ugolino rings horribly true:

> Having said this, with maddened eyes he seized
> that wretched skull again between his teeth
> and clenched them on the bone just like a dog. (33:76–78)

"So bestial a sign" indeed.

What does it matter, then, how we answer the question about literal cannibalism, which Dante has left, I'm claiming, intentionally ambiguous? He wants to suggest again that it's not so much a particular deed that is critical. What counts instead is the shape of a soul who has petrified his ability to sympathize even with those closest to him. Ugolino has the freedom to choose a life of fraudulent betrayal but is not free to escape its effects on his soul. These include the inability to summon tears when they are called for in the world above or the one below. The tercet above leaves us with as staggering a parting image as there is in *Inferno*: the likeness of a cannibal, regardless of what he has done.

Exercises

CLOSE READING

1. Rhyme. My students liked to respond to questions about how it functions. The tercet right above sets up a good one using the Italian itself. The first line ends with "torti," which describes Ugolino's eyes. The Hollanders translate "maddened," but a more literal translation would be "twisted." The rhyming third line ends with "forti," or "strong," which describes the doglike way he clamps down on Ruggieri's skull. Instead of translating the adjective *forti*, the Hollanders rely on the verb "clenched" to carry the idea of forceful tenacity. You could raise several related questions here. Since rhyme associates these two adjectives in our ear, you might ask what impression of Ugolino the rhymed pair, taken together, reinforces? Then your students might evaluate the translation in these two spots. What changes would they favor? Here's one of the few places where I think the Hollanders might be improved upon.
2. Repetition of key words. By the Hollanders' reckoning, "In this canto, vv. 5–75, words for weeping and grief (*piangere, lagrimare, doglia, dolere, dolore,* and *doloroso*) occur a total of thirteen times." Even though previous

characters in *Inferno* shed tears or seek sympathy, Ugolino carries these
tendencies much farther than others. Why all this emphasis in this canto
on this particular register of emotion? Part of an answer to this question
might focus on weeping's place in contrasting image patterns in canto
33. These contrasts get to the heart of what this canto is about, as I have
maintained above. If you agree with me, then your job is to get students to
see how meaningful ideas can be expressed through a contrast of images
without any editorial help. (No small undertaking.) Since the power of
this canto lies in Ugolino's narrative, its point must arise out of that. So the
question would be how the poet can use the contrast between tears and
stone to deepen understanding and sharpen evaluation of this character
and what he stands for.

A second approach to this question might look more critically into
what motivates Ugolino's long first-person narrative. He clearly intends for
his repeated appeals to stir up sympathy in pilgrim and guide. For whom?
I'm assuming it's obvious that the father deserves a lot less sympathy than
his sons. In his contemptuous apostrophe to the city of Pisa (33:79–90), the
poet implies that the sons were only innocent victims. Ugolino's numerous
references to weeping and grieving could then be seen as an attempt to blur
the distinction between objects of sympathy. To what end? The first blush
answer here—to gain some sympathy for himself—might not exhaust the
question. Psychologically, why all this emphasis on weeping and grief here
from a man who admits to having turned to stone, a man who admits that
for him "fasting had more power than grief?" Here's another place where
the poet deftly reveals more about a character than the character knows
about himself. That's not easy to do when your vehicle is the character's
own speech.

To demonstrate the difficulty of producing such ironic portraits, you
might assign it as a creative writing exercise. Have your students construct
a dramatic monologue with, say, a fellow classmate as speaker. Their first
job will be to produce a speech credible at a literal level—that is, classmates
will believe that it sounds like something the speaker might have said in
the given situation. At the same time, the speech will have to incriminate
the speaker, let's say comically, without his seeming to realize it. Presenting
these in class could be fun.

3. The syntax of Ugolino's famously ambiguous line 75: "Then fasting had
more power than grief." A look at the Italian (*Poscia, piu che 'l dolor, pote
'l digiuno*) will show your students how the Hollanders smoothed out a
broken line. Rendering the Italian as literally as possible in English would
give you "Then, more than grief, fasting had power." How artificial it seems

to place the lesser part of a "more than" comparison ahead of the greater, especially for someone at the emotional climax of his supposedly grief-stricken story. So what does the syntax of this line add to the characterization of its speaker? Does it help your students in evaluating Ugolino's appeals for sympathy? Has it any bearing on the question of whether Ugolino was literally a cannibal?

4. The poet's double use of apostrophe as a means to denounce cities. First Pisa (33:79–90), which Dante wishes would be flooded by the river Arno so as to "drown every living soul in you." Then Genoa, whose people he condemns as a "race estranged from every virtue, crammed with every vice," so much so that they should be "driven from the earth" (33:151–57). Don't these blanket denunciations of whole cities seem a little intemperate? I hope your students will find it hard to join the poet in the leap in generalizing condemnation from a villainous native son or two to an entire city. Emphasize that these are the poet's statements in present tense, not the pilgrim's. The strategy of directly addressing each city only calls attention to these cases of judgmental excess. If so, then what? If these passages, and maybe a few others, blast our confidence in the moral authority of the poet, is the poem ruined for us? Note that this is another version of the question I raised about the poet's depiction of Brunetto Latini in canto 15.

I can think of a few ways to try to squirm out of this conclusion. Maybe there is some kind of artistic justification for the two city apostrophes here. The condemnations of Pisa and Genoa might fit the patterns of this canto in ways that give them legitimacy. I confess to having a hard time getting very far down this path.

Perhaps these apostrophes are a reminder that a first-person narrator, even one who has been to paradise, is still human and subject to errors in judgment based on past conditioning. I'm guessing Florentines had a low opinion of both Pisa and Genoa, which conditioned response the poet is thoughtlessly expressing here. This, as I suggested in chapter 1, would add a dimension of depth and a kind of credibility to the poem that reading the narrator as the unfaltering spokesman for the author would lack. In dealing with divine things, would an infallible narrator really make sense?

Another way around the problem would be to ask your students how much they have to agree with an author's judgments to admire his work, or at least to suspend their disbelief long enough to give it a chance. This question has special force for a poem so avowedly judgmental as this one. Can your students tolerate a few lapses in judgment without that clouding their experience of the poem as a whole? Or can they separate the artistic from the moral dimension of the poem and love it enough as great art to override any moral, philosophical, or religious objections they have?

5.   The allusion mentioned above from the Gospel of Luke. Since fathers, sons, bread, and stone all figure prominently in the Luke passage and in Ugolino's story, the former probably does have some bearing on the latter. It's not easy to get your students to think hard enough for long enough to work out how the biblical passage sheds light on the *Inferno* one. But you may have trained them by now. If they do, their labor will certainly prove beneficial. They'll gain confidence in the value of close reading and in their own ability to savor some of that value.

THEMES AND ISSUES

1.   The giants stand firmly planted in an emblematic line from Cerberus through various figures like Plautus, the Minotaur, and Geryon. All these creatures act as representations, announcing what is to be found in the area over which they stand guard. What then do the giants, sentinels posted at the icy pit of hell, represent? Good answers will have to be consistent with the attributes Dante gives these huge figures, as well as with the imagery of deepest hell.

2.   You might prompt your students to use comparison to see Ugolino more clearly in characterization and/or artistic form. Have them pick one of the previous "persons" whom Dante develops along similar lines—Francesca, Farinata, Pier delle Vigne, Brunetto Latini, or Ulysses—to use as a means to shed new light on Dante's artistic methodology or on what distinguishes Ugolino from other *Inferno* figures. Similarities might sharpen their sense of how Dante the poet works and differences clarify what individualizes Ugolino.

3.   Virgil in canto 33. This may seem hard to give since Dante the poet gives Virgil very little. Virgil plays the slightest of roles here, speaking in only one tercet, in which he deflects a question by the pilgrim. Remembering how adept this poet is at communicating through absences, what would your students make of this one? Why does the poet imagine Virgil so conspicuously holding himself back here?

4.   A related question, one the poem sets up from the beginning: How are we to conceive the relationships among the three principal characters here? The pilgrim takes strong measures on his own regarding Ugolino and Fra Alberigo. Showing his mastery of the art of equivocation, he takes advantage of both these characters in order to trick them into telling their

stories. Neither the poet nor Virgil makes any comment on the pilgrim's unashamed manipulation in these cases.

You might employ the Skip Hays test here. A fiction writer who teaches in the MFA program at a university nearby, Skip used to visit my classes to talk about fiction. To come to final terms with a complex piece of fiction, he would say, you need to look for significant things that central characters do or say at the end of the work that they could not have said at the beginning. Answering this simple-looking question puts character development where it belongs: at the center of attempts to understand a work of literature. At the sizing-up-the-whole-work stage of a longer piece of reading, my students found Skip's approach helpful.

Here the pilgrim is showing what your students might call attitude. He seems independently capable of dealing with sinners in this canto, if we agree that misleading the damned constitutes acceptable behavior. He certainly seems to have left behind the guy who was cowering at the edge of the dark wood. Does the guide's backgrounding himself imply approval of the pilgrim's responses to Ugolino and Fra Alberigo? How would one argue this in either direction? Similarly for the poet: he has quite a bit to say in his own present-tense voice in this canto, but nothing that directly gauges the pilgrim's bold moves. (If anything, in his denunciations of Pisa and Genoa, he trumps the pilgrim pretty decisively in severity.) Is this a point in the poem where the pilgrim's maturation really begins to reveal itself? A place where the three principals are pretty much in accord? Or something less?

RESEARCH

1. Dante's negative-mirroring strategy. In some significant ways at least, he wants to structure the depths of hell as the reflective contrary of the heights of heaven, analogous to a photographic negative's relation to its print. He employs this device extensively in constructing hell's icy ninth circle. It culminates in his treatment of Satan in canto 34, but your students can begin to draw out the implications of Dante's structural logic here. What are the attributes of lower hell as the poet has pictured them so far? Dark and foggy, relatively quiet (the sounds of chattering teeth and an occasional voice versus the noisy wails and shrieks of upper hell), confining, cold, isolating, perhaps threatening in its eeriness, and maybe others you'll find. To feel the full force of this ensemble, your students would have to know something about Dante's depiction of heaven. By now, they might reasonably imagine Dante's idea of heaven to entail images counter

to those in the above list. But no abstracted imagining can substitute for looking closely at exactly what forms Dante's counterimages take. So have interested students read *Paradiso* with something like these questions in mind: Where in *Paradiso* do we find imagery and action in direct opposition to the icy final four cantos of *Inferno*? How can a detailed knowledge of heaven's counterimagery deepen our comprehension of the dark depths of hell's bottom?

Or you could turn this question in a Freccero direction. How would knowledge of the history, meaning, and practice of Christian communion ceremonies shed light on this canto? Where are the pertinent differences between the Eucharist and the cannibalism with which early Christians were charged? How should these differences affect our responses to Ugolino's sorrowful narrative?

11

Dis

CANTO 34

Recall that the pilgrim's dominant emotion in canto 1 was fear. Virgil's original job description must have italicized the need to alleviate that fear. Notice how Virgil's guidance has now started to bear fruit. Despite some understandable backsliding with the giants, you'd have to conclude that the pilgrim's interactions with hell dwellers have grown increasingly bold and self-assured, leaving Virgil with little role to play in cantos 32 and 33, for better or worse. This should make sense plot-wise as the pilgrim's infernal education takes hold. Though the sentinel monsters and demons can sometimes seem frightening (until Virgil's connection to divine authority sweeps them aside), the damned finally aren't very scary.

In canto 34, Dante's characterization of Satan functions as culminating and comprehensive testimony to that claim. The pilgrim certainly fears Satan here, but how frightening does he loom objectively? I hope you'll say "not very." He doesn't really loom at all, but languishes more pathetically than fearfully. Though he is still sufficiently huge and powerful to inflict great damage on anyone who comes under his influence, he no longer gets any pleasure out of it. Instead, his malice is the source of his own torment, so much so that "Out of his six eyes he wept and his three chins/dripped tears and drooled blood-red saliva" (33:53–54). This is not a happy archrebel. None of his rebellious bravado remains here. That destructive nature that once seemed liberating he now experiences as torturous confinement.

But the most telling idea expressed in Dante's description of Satan concerns the cause of his icy immobility:

> . . . When he flapped them [his wings],
> he sent forth three separate winds,
> the sources of the ice upon Cocytus. (33:50–52)

However faulty Dante's meteorology, the idea here is profound. By flapping his six wings, Satan makes his own ice! And thus, "he is fit to be the source of every sorrow" (33:36). In his hubristic attempt to supersede his creator, Satan has turned a state of being that was ."fair" and full of possibility into something "hideous." Aren't all the sorrows above in hell marked by some of this prideful satanic egocentrism, compounded with one corrupted human potential or another? Pride can turn natural appetite into blameworthy incontinence, natural aggressiveness into culpable violence, and natural dexterity of mind into cunning fraudulence. The result: souls so dominated by a faculty out of control that they lose the good of intellect and have no real hope of repenting.

You have to wonder when ice-making begins. When do souls begin to narrow their perspective, giving away their expansive natural (or God-given) freedom for various increasingly confining pseudo-rewards? Surely not just after they die. Even before they died, weren't all the damned making their own ice, i.e. their own powerful winds, flaming coffins, twisted bodies, flaming tongues, immersions in excrement, or cannibalistic appetites? Satan's must have been an icy soul even before he fell from heaven to create the geography of hell. Taken broadly, God's contrapasso acts in this way. For my money, Satan's frozen situation in the pit of hell really nails this claim down.

What's the appropriate response to those souls in whom this process has petrified itself, those that are trapped forever in the torment they have made for themselves? Surely not fear. Predictably, in beholding Satan for the first time, the pilgrim reacts according to his conditioning:

> Then how faint and frozen I became,
> reader, do not ask, for I do not write it,
> since any words would fail to be enough.
>
> I did not die, nor did I stay alive.
> Imagine, if you have the wit,
> what I became, deprived of both. (34:22–27)

What is at first great fear quickly modulates into something else, some mysterious state between life and death. The poet is attempting here to characterize the pilgrim at a turning point, positioned on the brink of a kind of new birth. After these two tercets, nothing more is made of the pilgrim's fear. Instead the poet supplies a largely expository description of what the pilgrim sees, like what a tour guide might point out. Virgil's commentary is even more matter-of-fact: he covers the torments of the three gnawees, Judas, Brutus, and Cassius, in three cursory tercets and is then quite abruptly ready to leave. It's as if the pilgrim's short semester in hell should have taught him not to make too much of this scene, not to want to gawk at Satan, not to see this place as any climax to the horrors of hell. By now, Satan's condition here should seem immediately intelligible to the pilgrim. Understanding ought to begin to trump conditioned patterns of emotion in him.

Instead of pausing to reflect, Virgil takes appropriate action. Here again, Dante communicates his greatest profundities through images without editorial comment. As with Geryon in canto 17, the only way forward here is through using the demonic as a vehicle. In fact in both places Dante uses the same word, *scale*, which the Hollanders render "stairs" in canto 17 and "rungs" here. In either case, the image is of something to be climbed over toward a destination. Far from getting to circumvent Satan on the way up to purgatory, the pilgrim has to experience his beastly flanks intimately from Virgil's back as his guide climbs handful by hairy handful down Satan's body. Once again, you transcend sin, in this case the archetype of sin, not by just avoiding it but by coming to understand its true nature up close. Satan here unwittingly serves a beneficial function in the poem: as a ladder, not an obstacle.

Then the poet has to submit to his own cosmological logic. As guide and pilgrim descend feet first down Satan's body, they must soon reach to its center, "where the thighbone swivels, at the broad part of the hips." I'm not sure exactly what part of Satan's body is indicated here, but perhaps the reference is to Satan's privates. If so, appropriately. The epicenter of malign counterfertility lies here. As with many other details in Satan's description, this imagery evokes its heavenly contrary, in this case in God's creative power.

If poet and pilgrim were to continue to climb in the same direction past this center of gravity, they would be ascending feet first. Already Virgil as an insubstantial shade has to carry Dante's fleshy body on his back. To force him to do so acrobatically would be cruel punishment indeed. Therefore

. . . my leader with much strain of limb and breath,

turned his head where Satan had his shanks
and clung to the hair like a man climbing upward,
so that I thought we were heading back to Hell. (33:78–81)

This dramatic image of turning around works as well in theological as physical terms. Any case for Canto 34 as the climax of *Inferno* would have to emphasize this moment of turning. Think of the meaning of that verb, "to turn," in Christian theology, especially as it relates to the encounter with Satan. (The *close* encounter with Satan. I insist that there is profundity in this image.) But notice how the poet almost immediately undercuts any sense of climactic high seriousness in this scene. The Satan the two of them have traversed now looks from a

little distance like the pitiful upside down figure that the pilgrim should understand him to be, a fitting denouement for a being who epitomizes making your
own suffering. With his legs in the air, not horrible, not clever, not masterful or
even very formidable, but misdirected, ignorant, pitiful, even a little ridiculous.
That should now seem to be just Virgilian good sense. All of the pilgrim's education in *Inferno* has pointed to this prosaic realization. Now all Virgil's talk bends
toward the next stage of the pilgrim's journey, and ours.

Exercises

Since you should be well acquainted with my approaches to fostering close
reading—unpacking similes, chasing down allusions, discovering meaningful
rhymes, and so on—I'll dispense with that category here. Besides, canticle's end
should engage the sweeping more than the pinpointed gaze, don't you think?
Instead, I'll frame several broad questions about canto 34 followed by a few dealing with the *Inferno* as a whole.

CANTO 34

1. In canto 34, according to the Hollanders (34:37–38n), Satan "stands before
    us as a parodic version of Christ crucified." Though I'm not sure parody is
    the right term for what the poet is doing here, he certainly constructs his
    picture of Satan at many points as a counterpoint to Christ and the divine.
    This culminates Dante's structural project that has been gaining force over
    the last two cantos: when you approach the spatial antithesis of heaven in
    the poem, you find it structured around negative reflections of heavenly
    images. The poet implicitly encourages his readers to think of heaven in
    trying to understand the depths of hell. So where are these correspon-
    dences in canto 34 and what does the poet gain out of the broad strategy
    that comes to a head here? Why would Dante have you hear any echo at
    all of heavenly things in the last few cantos of *Inferno*? You could start by
    investigating the allusion to an ancient Christian hymn at the beginning of
    this canto.
2. Suppose that the encounter with Satan is the culminating expression of
    the poet's thought on the subject of punishment. If so, what responses
    to the damned would he endorse? Should the damned be pitied? If not,
    what? Literally, I find the poet's position on this question hard to swallow
    whole. The pilgrim has learned that the damned are not to be pitied, that
    he can use them fearlessly as needed to further his journey, and that he can

justifiably treat them harshly when he likes. Have there been exceptions? Almost anyone who reads the poem finds a few, I think, which may make the poet's medicine go down a little easier.

But allegorically, at the level of *our* journey where his poem in effect claims universal application, his case seems more compelling. Because each of the damned represents an area of negative potential in any human soul, hard-nosed antipathy leading to proper restraint of each destructive possibility might yield a healthier, better-ordered soul than pity will. But restraint should not be identified with mere avoidance. During their descent, the guide has repeatedly had to turn the pilgrim's head toward hell's inhabitants. To continue the journey upward from the pit of hell in canto 34, Dante and Virgil have to climb Satan's body like a ladder with the hair on his coat for handholds. Apparently, the damnable potentials in the soul are to be acknowledged, faced up to, and learned from, not just circumvented or pushed back into the muck, repressively. No canto makes that point more memorably than this one. What are the implications, for understanding and behavior, of this imagery? Make your students get down to attitudes and actions that they believe Dante would support. Don't let them lose sight of that troublesome *our*.

3. Similarly for the imagery of turning around. Christian thinking is linear and (therefore?) climactic: biblical history and the journeys of individual believers hinge on certain well-defined turning points. Perhaps because the life of the Christian spirit is conceived as a journey, the New Testament overflows with images of movement to express man's relation to God, with turning away and turning toward occurring most frequently. You could say that proper turning becomes pivotal. What, then, is the significance of the turning point in this canto, marked by the imagery of turning around on Satan's body at the center of gravity of the universe, and resulting in a new direction for pilgrim and guide?

4. Consider tone in canto 34. You will have seen how Dante sometimes likes to complicate conditioned cultural or religious expectations. Canto 34 affords further evidence of this strategy. He colors the Prince of Darkness here in much less forbidding hues than conventions would lead you to expect. Horror and repulsion shade almost into *pathos*, or maybe *bathos*. Where you would have expected an emotional peak, you get a matter-of-fact attitude tinged with ridicule. Compared to Ugolino, the characterization of Satan here strikes me as anticlimactic. If so, it's artistically risky. Usually considered an artistic flaw, anticlimax has to serve some purpose here important enough to justify the risk of undermining the significance of the ending. What does the poet gain by this treatment of Satan that

more than counterbalances the risk of being accused of emotional misdirection? Why does the tempering of emotion here not mar the last canto of *Inferno*?

5.   Maybe the poet's problem here is tone management. The poet doesn't leave himself many lines to transport readers from Satan's icy darkness to a view of the stars, those reflections of divine light and signs of God's highly ordered cosmos. Moving pilgrim and guide too abruptly from a horrible encounter with the archdemon to the happiness of looking upon such stars might strain readers' credibility and tax them emotionally. How to smooth out that transition a little? More negotiable is the emotional curve the poem actually does trace from fear through dispassionate factual reportage and calm, distanced evaluation up to happiness.

Here might be the place to raise questions whose real function is to remind your students that the *Inferno* is part of the *Commedia*. The Hollanders' note on the canto's last line may be helpful:

> . . . in this line both Virgil and Dante actually step out of hell, and now can see the full expanse of the dawn sky filled with stars. Both *Purgatorio* and *Paradiso* will also end with the word "stars" (*stelle*), the goals of a human sight that is being drawn to God. There is no doubt as to the fact that even *Inferno*, ending in happiness of this kind, is a comedic part of a comedic whole. (33:139n.)

So Dante uses "stars" as the last word of all three canticles as signals of a comedic intention. Earlier, I followed Northrop Frye (2000) in claiming that literary comedy might entail not just any happy ending but one that depends on the ultimate reintegration of the hero into his environment, in some sense. (It might help to remember here that the *Commedia* is the work of an exile who can never go home to Florence again.) You could raise questions about how far the Hollanders are right in calling this ending comedic and about emotional management in a great work of literary art. How much does the poet's desire to make the ending feel positive affect his handling of Satan earlier in the canto? How would they evaluate the emotional effectiveness of the culminating last canto of *Inferno*? Get them to thinking about how great writers orchestrate emotion satisfyingly.

6.

Fire and Ice
by Robert Frost

Some say the world will end in fire,
Some say in ice.
From what I've tasted of desire
I hold with those who favor fire.

> But if it had to perish twice,
> I think I know enough of hate
> To say that for destruction ice
> Is also great
> And would suffice.

Would you need to substitute "pride" for "hate" here or are the two terms close enough kin that the modern poem can stand as a commentary on the old one? On what points would Frost seem to agree with Dante? Where would he take issue?

THE INFERNO AS A WHOLE

1. How have his experiences in the underworld affected the pilgrim? There are several other good ways to frame this question. In terms of the relationship between pilgrim and poet or pilgrim and guide: how has that changed? In terms of the Skip Hays question: what does the pilgrim do, say, or think toward the end of the poem that he couldn't have at the beginning? How are those differences significant? Any of these variations should require students to hold up for comparison pairs of specific passages from the text, early and late, and to explain how their difference matters in understanding what Dante is up to in *Inferno* as a whole.

2. Can we assume that, for Dante, Virgil stands literally as the best of pagan mentors and allegorically as the wisest, most virtuous character that humans can achieve on their own powers, unaided by divine revelation and Christian teaching? If so, then taking the *Inferno* as a whole, what are the qualities of a great pagan teacher? How far can we humans get by fully developing our natural powers, particularly our rational ones? Where would Dante find limitations? According to this canticle, how would the poet finally evaluate the guide who has brought the pilgrim so far from the dark wood?

3. More generally, how does a great medieval poet (and I'd say philosopher), steeped in classical learning, evaluate the great pagan Greek and Roman thinkers? In what ways would Dante's attitude toward them differ from those of contemporary Christians your students know or have read? How fair would your students say his treatment of them is? As I have said, these were the questions that first brought me to Dante. I have to say that I find in this poem a broader-minded, more knowledgeable, and hence thoughtful treatment of the pagans than in almost any Christian apologist I have read on this subject.

4. The idea that Dante Alighieri's journey in 1300 can at the same time be "our journey" pushes you toward allegory. At the very least, the poem's first line implies we must share some common human attributes with the pilgrim and must eventually move through something similar to the landscape described in the *Inferno*. One obvious way to solve the problem this "our" creates is to see the pilgrim as representing the reflexive possibility in every human soul and touring hell as the chance to reflect upon the soul's own architecture. By descending through the circles of hell and surveying the damned, pilgrim and reader get an education in the essential construction of any soul. Through seeing all the ways a soul can go wrong, we learn how a soul is structured and where its potentials lie. If so, then *Inferno* above all is Dante's blueprint for what a soul in the universal is and what divine causalities affect its experience.

    What, then, would Dante have your students learn about souls whose makeup can generate wrongdoing in three general beastly categories, whose compartments can from one side be represented by Francesca, Pier della Vigna, Ulysses, Ugolino, and Satan himself, not to forget Virgil, and whose behavior is governed by the contrapasso, in the next life, and, I've maintained, in this one? What, according to Dante, is the nature of this divinely created essence of what we all are?

5. Dante's main premise tackled broadly. Any way you read the poem, you find the assumption that God has established in his creation an order that is moral, salvific, and not immediately visible. Modern secularists would require evidence to support any such claims. Ask your students whether they believe in any kind of invisible moral order with the power to affect the lives of human beings. What evidence or arguments can they supply for any affirmative answers? You may find that he question naturally divides along the boundary separating this world from the next. The latter dimension, if it is one, may not give you very interesting results. Obviously, contentions based on religious authority work if you accept the authority but not if you don't. They may posit effects in the next life that your nonbelievers will have no logical reason to accept. You may, though, get some pragmatic arguments that are interesting and at least potentially testable— for example, that believing in an afterlife of rewards and punishments contributes to a better life before death. Such applications of the idea of an invisible order to life in this world are likely to be much more broadly effective in classroom conversation.

    I read Dante as affirming some such order. (Along with quite a few other major writers. Put Dostoevsky, for example, on the list, if *Crime and Punishment* is your evidence. By the way, teaching that novel next to *Inferno* can work very well for you in the classroom.) Here's one way to help students bring this inquiry out of fiction and into the world of their experience. Ask them whether it is possible to do really terrible things in the world and get completely away with them. Obviously it is possible in external terms. People do get away with heinous crimes. Does the inner life offer the same possibility? Not apparently for Dante the pilgrim, who was at the pinnacle of worldly fame and power when he awoke to find himself in a dark wood, almost beyond saving. (Nor for Raskolnikov, under a similar, but not identical, order.) But a student's agreement with great writers like these should count for little without some argument classmates could evaluate.

6. The inscription above the gates of hell. Let's judge Dante's God by his own standards:

JUSTICE MOVED MY MAKER ON HIGH.
DIVINE POWER MADE ME,
WISDOM SUPREME, AND PRIMAL LOVE. (3:4–6)

The playing field for evaluating these words will sprawl too much without at least one ground rule to narrow it down. If your students accept provisionally God's creative architecture in the poem, how would Dante argue for the creator's transcendent power, justice, wisdom, and love? Allow them to set up no straw Dantes here. Once they have framed the poet's arguments as strongly as possible, they will have laid the foundation for debating how convincing Dante's implicit picture of God is. On Dante's terms, power is no problem. The divine architect of the *Commedia*'s universe had to have exercised great power. Students may well find the other three terms thorny. Particularly the last.

7. Consider pride, the arch-sin. Why would Christians designate it as that? Positing Satan's rebellion as the answer won't suffice here because it only leads to a further question. What is it about Satan's prideful rebellion against God that makes it fundamental to what sin is to Christians, such that it underlies all other sins? I think Satanic mythology does make an important point here, especially if you consider the problem of sin to stem from the problem of self. In a Christian scheme, with the idea of pride as a guide, how should a self understand her own position in relation to the creator, to other human agents, and to the rest of the creation? This may be one of those questions that generate an answer that is easy to conceptualize but devilishly hard to live out.

An eccentricity in the English language doesn't make things any easier. We use one word to cover a lot of diverse terrain. As a parent or teacher, you might follow Christian teaching in warning the youth in your life against the ultimate dangers of pride. In my family we called that the bad pride. You have to somehow square that with encouragement you might give to your charges to have pride in their school or their team or their own appearance and accomplishments. That was the good pride. What is a child to do about the confusion surrounding this word? How is she to distinguish between the two kinds of pride in actual situations she confronts on her own, when wise parental guidance is not available? Is there a way to distinguish pride as a virtue from pride as a sin while maintaining enough of a relationship between the two sides to justify their placement under the same linguistic umbrella?

I guess what is called for here is a piece of linguistic analysis. That might prove a useful exercise in itself, but I'm betting if it interests you, you'll find livelier ways to turn students' attention to this vexing problem, so morally fundamental to Christian thinking.

8.   One more look at that brazen *our*.

I hope I have convinced you that you need to include *Inferno* in your syllabus. The list of reasons why runs out to some length, as I hope this book has shown. The poem's established position up among the Himalayan peaks of literary greatness constitutes reason enough, of course. But I have been trying to emphasize its pragmatic value to high-school literature teachers. It works in the classroom. Though your functionality standards are no doubt different from mine, this poem can support a great range of classroom purposes. There's something in it for any literature teacher. At least, that's my faith.

As history rolled itself out in the last few decades, I began to try to fill my syllabus with works that shared one particular virtue: the ability to stimulate students to talk their way around culturally conditioned barriers separating them from people around them. This became my main measure of utility. As I have said earlier, Dante's poem consistently graded out very high under this standard. The *Inferno*'s gutsy first line *nostra* announces Dante's intention: "I'm about to demonstrate, reader, how my journey can be at the same time yours and everyone else's. How there are essential features common to all human paths of life in all places and times." That would pose a bit of a challenge.

How successful is he in meeting it? Based on their scrutiny of the first third of the *Commedia*, where are the features of the pilgrim's journey that your students would agree to universalize? In terms of the human journey from cradle to grave, what common ground has Dante marked out for us that Christians, Muslims, Jews, Buddhists, agnostics, atheists, animists, and even Unitarians can share? What universal turnings in our path would they say the poet has failed to map?

Extension: Dante and the Visual Arts

The history of illustration of the *Commedia* is so long and rich that it would seem a shame not to make some use of it in the classroom. The lengthy list of illustrators includes such luminaries as Sandro Botticelli, William Blake, and Gustave Dore. Several recent editions of *Inferno* feature memorable sets of illustrations, my favorite being Barry Moser's in the Mandelbaum (1981) edition. Working up an activity for your students based on the visual arts may require some extra legwork for you in gathering materials, but I think you will find that the results justify your labors. My students really seemed to enjoy any activity I could devise using illustrations of *Inferno* cantos. You'll probably be able to think of more creative ways to use these materials in the classroom than I did, but I'm guessing that they'll be based on one or the other of two related considerations. Accuracy: how faithful is a given illustration to the relevant material in the text as your student reads it? Interpretation: how does a particular artistic image construe the text? Comparisons worked very well with my students, too. Which of these two artistic renditions of Satan in canto 34 does a better job of illustrating what Dante actually says about Satan there? How do these two illustrations of the dark wood in canto 1 differ interpretively? You may also find that your more artistically gifted students will relish the opportunity to produce *Inferno* imagery of their own.

A Canticle-Sized Extension: An Updated *Inferno*

The idea is to update *Inferno* by expanding it to cover modern transgressions that a medieval poet would have had no way to consider. Many instances of this kind of adaptation exist. I remember one funny one published in the *Village Voice* some years ago with something like "Hades of the Eighties" in the title. You won't have to work hard to find that or something like it to use as a model to inspire your students.

Student writing here could simply take the form of a piece of prose describing a modern sin and outlining a contrapasso appropriate to it. But I found it amusing to sharpen the requirements in various ways based on how close to *Inferno* I wanted students to hew.

Step 1 in that direction: dovetailing. They would have to find an appropriate place inside *Inferno*'s logical structure into which to insert their selected sin.

Since *Inferno* claims complete coverage of the infernal region, any adaptation would have to respect *Inferno*'s broad categories. So whatever sins your students identify should, theoretically at least, be classifiable as incontinent, violent, or fraudulent. If that turns out to be feasible, it's a pretty impressive accomplishment for a piece of seven-hundred-year-old taxonomy.

Step 2: But with placement, greater precision is better. Maybe a chosen modern sin should be located *within* a given canto. Defending such a placement would require a closer piece of analysis of Dante's intentions. That has to be a good thing.

Step 3: Then you could require them to compose their insert so that it not only fits logically in a particular place but sits seamlessly between two particular Dante lines.

Step 4: Then you might encourage them to compose in poetry, the closer to terza rima, the better. This may seem daunting, but my students loved trying to work within a poetic form, often for their first time. They would have little trouble forming rhyming tercets (usually axa, byb, czc, etc., but I remember a few audacious attempts at full terza rima). Rarely, though, did they form rhymes while maintaining anything very close to the iambic pentameter line. To make the rhymes work, their lines would sometimes run out to fifteen syllables or more. Still, I think they learned a lot from this, not just about Dante but about the challenges (and pleasures) of trying to fit their thinking to the requirements of a fixed poetic form. Regardless of how close they got, we always had a good time presenting the results in class.

Step 5: Then you could require them to add to their insertion some of the apparatus that editions of *Inferno* typically provide: informational and maybe interpretive notes. Most editions include both, maybe prefaced by a brief road-map summary of the sort that Ciardi (2001) gives before each canto. Again, this may sound demanding. But the one year I extended the rules this far, I got good results and good reviews from my students on the worth of the exercise. They enjoyed playing Dante for a little while.

APPENDIX 1

Editions of *Inferno*

The annotated list below is far from exhaustive. It comprises those available English language editions of the poem with which I am familiar. It's hard to keep up: one source lists twenty-five English translations of *Inferno* since Dorothy Sayers's in 1950. Other worthy editions I have not cited are certainly out there. I feel a little presumptuous in evaluating the work of these noted translators, several of them also renowned poets, but I justify this effort by reminding myself that high school teachers do have to make their textbook choices. I hope to provide you some help in doing that.

Scholarly Editions

Durling, Robert M., and Ronald Martinez, trans. *Inferno*. By Dante Alighieri. Oxford University Press, 1997.

> A single-volume translation in accessible prosy verse with Italian on the facing page. Features a very thorough introduction, helpful maps and illustrations, good scholarly notes canto by canto, and an "Additional Notes" section at the end with a number of short interpretive essays on specific cantos. As with the Hollanders' edition, this might not be the version you'd choose to provide high-school students their first taste of the poem, but it could serve you and them admirably as a vehicle for deeper delving.

Hollander, Robert, and Jean Hollander, trans. *Inferno*. By Dante Alighieri. Anchor, 2002.

> A fairly recent single-volume edition by a husband-and-wife team; she, a poet, does most of the composing—in verse, tercets but no terza rima; he, a scholar, is mainly responsible for the notes, which are both informative and interpretive. I'd rank them as good or better than Sayers's, which is saying something. The result: a great piece of work on both poetic and scholarly counts. Comes in an affordable paperback version. My favorite edition of the poem, though it may offer many high-school students more than they are ready to receive.

Musa, Mark, trans. *Inferno*. By Dante Alighieri. Indiana University Press, 1997.

> A two-volume edition with volume one including a revised version of his original (1995) verse translation with added Italian on the facing page, and volume two consisting of a greatly expanded interpretive commentary.

Though I find Musa's interpretive remarks on Inferno uneven, they are often very helpful. Again probably too expensive for general classroom use.

Singleton, Charles S., trans. *Inferno*. By Dante Alighieri. Princeton University Press, 1990.

In two volumes, with a prose translation with Italian facing page in one volume, lengthy commentary in the other. Translation is as literal as you will find. You may surprise yourself at how much Italian you can make out with its help. Commentary is primarily informative rather than interpretive; it tries to make accessible to English speakers all the materials needed to do original research on the *Inferno*. Almost indispensable to serious study of the poem, but its cost will probably relegate it to use as a classroom resource rather than primary textbook status.

Shorter Single-Volume Editions

Ciardi, John, trans. *Inferno*. By Dante Alighieri. Signet, 2001.

A famous poet's verse translation with a partial stab at terza rima by rhyming first and third lines of each tercet—often pads the English line to hold line numbers and syllable counts consistent with Italian; notes and canto summaries make this the most accessible edition of *Inferno*, but at a cost of some simplistic assertions. Maybe the most affordable edition available; hence the one I used in class for many years and found on the whole quite satisfactory.

Lombardo, Stanley, trans. *Inferno*. By Dante Alighieri. Hackett, 2009.

The most recent edition here by a celebrated translator of Homer, famous for breathing new life into the *Iliad* and the *Odyssey*; the trademark vigor of his translations due in part to a distinctive intention: to produce a translation suitable for oral presentation, as with the two Homeric epics; approximates Dante's verse form in meter but without rhyme; thorough explanatory (versus interpretive) notes and an illuminating introduction; a solid choice, though a little more costly than Ciardi or Mandelbaum.

Mandelbaum, Allen, trans. *Inferno*. By Dante Alighieri. Quality Paperback Books, 1981.

A renowned translator's lively translation with Italian facing, sketchy notes in back, features superb illustrations by Barry Moser, and is quite inexpensive.

Musa, Mark, trans. *Inferno*. By Dante Alighieri. Indiana University Press, 1995

An unrhymed verse translation with good notes.

Pinsky, Robert, trans. *The Inferno of Dante*. By Dante Alighieri. Farrar, Straus, and Giroux, 1993.

The former poet laureate's verse translation is like Ciardi's, but with no padding so that you end up with fewer English lines than Italian ones in each canto (it generally takes fewer syllables to say something in English than in Italian), Italian on facing page, brief notes in back are occasionally helpful but the occasional paragraph-length canto introductions by RP (Robert Pinsky) and especially JF (John Freccero) are usually brilliant. Freccero's introduction to the whole volume is itself worth the price of admission. Can be found in an inexpensive version.

Sayers, Dorothy L., trans. *The Divine Comedy, Part 1: Hell.* By Dante Alighieri. Penguin, 1950.

An older verse translation in full terza rima (the inability of such a renowned writer and Dante scholar to pull this off very successfully is indicative of how impossible a task this is in English); her notes and introduction, however, are extremely helpful.

APPENDIX 2

Online Resources

Sites Serving You and Your Students Broadly

World of Dante (http://www.worldofdante.org): the most comprehensive of sites in this category in what it offers: "to facilitate the study of the *Divine Comedy.*" Features most importantly an Italian text with English translation for each canto linked to a variety of supplementary enrichment materials that are copious, detailed, and accessible. Also includes a gallery of images, access to Dante-inspired music, maps of textual geography, a timeline concentrating on text-related events during Dante's lifetime (1265–1321) and an extensive "Teacher Resources" section. An impressively thoroughgoing multimedia research tool.

Danteworlds (http://danteworlds.laits.utexas.edu): a very accessible site empha-sizing a gallery of visual images illustrating features of each circle of *Inferno* (likewise for the major divisions of *Purgatorio* and *Paradiso*) integrated with notes on the written text, audio readings of selected lines in Italian, and study questions. Some students will find the visual orientation here appealing.

Dante Today: Citings and Sighting of Dante and His Works in Contemporary Culture: (http://research.bowdoin.edu/dante today): collects references to Dante and his works in modern and contemporary culture (over the last century or so). Highly inclusive—contains material across the spectrum from scholarly to popular; categories vary from "Written Word," "Visual Arts and Architecture," and "Performing Arts" to "Consumer Goods," "Dining and Leisure," "Music," "Places," and "Odds and Ends." Features a handy "Teaching Resources" section. Connections with popular arts might help interest a broader range of students in the study of *Inferno*.

Sites Serving More Scholarly Interests

Below are three renowned sites for doing line-by-line scholarly research on the *Divine Comedy*.

The Princeton Dante Project (http://etcweb.princeton.edu/dante/index.html): constructed around the Hollanders' translation of the *Divine Comedy*, but includes links to Toynbee's *Dante Dictionary* as well as translations of Dante's minor works. Search tool looks for particular words or strings of words in the text and provides access to Hollander's commentary as well as entrees in Toynbee's (1920) dictionary. Site also includes some Hollander lectures and philological notes in addition to a variety of multimedia imagery. Very useful if you like the Hollanders' approach, as I do.

The Dartmouth Dante Project (https://dante.dartmouth.edu): a search tool linking any line of the *Divine Comedy* to any in a long list of specific commentaries ranging in time from 1322 to 2015, many in Italian, some in Latin and English.

The Dante Lab at Dartmouth College (http://dantelab.dartmouth.edu): links individual lines of text in Italian and English to "700 years worth of [scholarly] commentaries." Rearranges Dartmouth Dante Project materials in a potentially more useful form.

BIBLIOGRAPHY

Auden, W. H. *The Living Thoughts of Kierkegaard*. McKay, 1952.

Bloom, Harold. *The Anxiety of Influence*. Oxford University Press, 1997.

Booth, Wayne, ed. *The Knowledge Most Worth Having*. University of Chicago Press, 2006.

Chadwick, Henry, trans. Confessions. By Saint Augustine. Oxford University Press, 2009.

Ciardi, John, trans. Inferno. By Dante Alighieri. Signet, 2001.

Cleary, Thomas, ed. *The Essential Koran*. Harper, 1994.

Clough, Arthur Hugh, ed., and John Dryden, trans. *Plutarch's Lives* vol. 2. By Plutarch. Modern Library, 1992.

Corley, Corin, trans. *Lancelot of the Lake*. Oxford University Press, 2008.

Day Lewis, C., trans. *The Aeneid*. By Virgil. Anchor, 1953.

———. *The "Eclogues" and "Georgics."* By Virgil. Oxford University Press, 2009.

Durling, Robert M., trans. Inferno. By Dante Alighieri. Oxford University Press, 1997.

English Standard Version Study Bible. Crossway, 2008.

Fagles, Robert, trans. *The Oresteia*. By Aeschylus. Penguin, 1984.

———. *The Three Theban Plays*. By Sophocles. Penguin, 1984.

Fox, Matthew, trans. *Civil War*. By Lucan. Penguin, 2012.

Freccero, John. *Dante: The Poetics of Conversion*. Harvard University Press, 1986.

Frye, Northrop. *Anatomy of Criticism: Four Essays*. Princeton University Press, 2000.

Fussell, Paul. *Poetic Meter and Poetic Form*. McGraw-Hill, 1979.

Golding, William. *Lord of the Flies*. Capricorn Books, 1954.

Graves, Robert. *The Greek Myths*. Penguin, 1993.

Greenblatt, Stephen. *The Swerve*. Norton, 2012.

Hollander, Robert and Jean Hollander, trans. Inferno. By Dante Alighieri. Anchor, 2002.

———. Purgatorio. By Dante Alighieri. Anchor, 2004.

———. Paradiso. By Dante Alighieri. Anchor 2008.

Holy Bible: King James Version. American Bible Society, 1980.

Hornblower, Simon, Antony Spawforth, and Esther Eidinow, eds. *Oxford Classical Dictionary,* 4th ed. Oxford University Press, 2012.

Lee, Desmond, trans. *Republic*. By Plato. Penguin, 2003.

Lewis, C. S. *Mere Christianity*. Harper, 2009.

Lombardo, Stanley, trans. *Iliad*. By Homer. Hackett, 1997.

————. *Inferno.* By Dante Alighieri. Hackett, 2009.

————. *Odyssey.* By Homer. Hackett, 2000.

Mandelbaum, Allen, trans. Inferno. By Dante Alighieri. Bantam, 1982.

————. Inferno. By Dante Alighieri. Quality Paperback Books, 1981.

Musa, Mark, trans. Inferno. By Dante Alighieri. Indiana University Press, 1995.

————. Inferno, Vols. 1 & 2. By Dante Alighieri. Indiana University Press, 1997.

————. Vita Nuova. By Dante Alighieri. Oxford University Press, 2008.

New International Version Holy Bible. Zonerdvan, 2012.

O'Connor, Flannery. *Three by Flannery O'Connor.* Signet Classics, 1986.

Pinsky, Robert, trans. Inferno. By Dante Alighieri. Farrar, Straus, and Giroux, 1993.

Singleton, Charles, trans. Inferno, Part 1 (text). By Dante Alighieri. Princeton University Press, 1990.

————. Inferno, Part 2 (commentary). Princeton University Press, 1990.

Sayers, Dorothy L., trans. The Divine Comedy, Part I: Hell. By Dante Alighieri. Penguin, 1950.

Spitzer, Leo. "Speech and Language in Inferno XIII," *Italica* 29 (Sept 1942): 81–104.

Stallings, Alicia, trans. *The Nature of Things.* By Lucretius. Penguin, 2007.

Stanford, W. B. *The Ulysses Theme.* Spring Publications, 2000.

Tarrant, Harold, ed., and Hugh Tredennick, trans. *The Last Days of Socrates.* By Plato. Penguin, 2003.

Toynbee, Paget. *Dantis Alagherii Epistolae. The Letters of Dante. Emended Text, with Introduction, Translation, Notes and Indices, and Appendix on the Cursus.* Clarendon Press, 1920.

Trilling, Lionel. *Beyond Culture.* Penguin, 1967.

Vonnegut, Kurt. *Cat's Cradle.* Dial Press, 2006.

————. *Slaughterhouse-Five.* Dell, 1990

Wolff, Tobias. *In Pharoah's Army.* Vintage, 1995.

INDEX